Fifty Hikes
in Eastern
Pennsylvania

Fifty Hikes in Eastern Pennsylvania

Day Hikes and Backpacks From the Susquehanna to the Poconos

Carolyn Hoffman

Photographs by the Author

Backcountry
Publications, Inc.
Woodstock, Vt.

An Invitation to the Reader

Developments, logging, and fires all take their toll on hiking
trails, often from one year to the next. If you find that
conditions along these fifty hikes have changed, please let
the author and publisher know so that corrections may be made in
future editions. Address all correspondence:

Editor, *Fifty Hikes*
Backcountry Publications, Inc.
Woodstock, Vermont 05091

Acknowledgments

Many of these hikes were suggested by employees of the Pennsylvania
Department of Environmental Resources, primarily in the Bureau of
Forestry. They proposed hikes and access routes, and provided
much historical and geographical information. Their help to me
and to the trails in Pennsylvania is gratefully acknowledged.
    I also want to thank Marilyn Wilderson, my editor, for her
help and patience.

Library of Congress Cataloging in Publication Data

Hoffman, Carolyn.
    Fifty hikes in eastern Pennsylvania.

    (The Fifty hikes series)
    1. Hiking—Pennsylvania—Guide-books.   2. Backpacking
—Pennsylvania—Guide-books.   3. Pennsylvania—
Description and travel—1951-   —Guide-books.
I. Title.   II. Series.
GV199.42.P4H63   917.48   82-4004
ISBN 0-942440-02-1 (pbk.)   AACR2

Published by Backcountry Publications, Inc.
Woodstock, Vermont
Printed in the United States of America
Design by Wladislaw Finne
Trail maps drawn by Cathy Camp.

To my family,
who mostly aren't hikers and
To my friends,
who mostly are

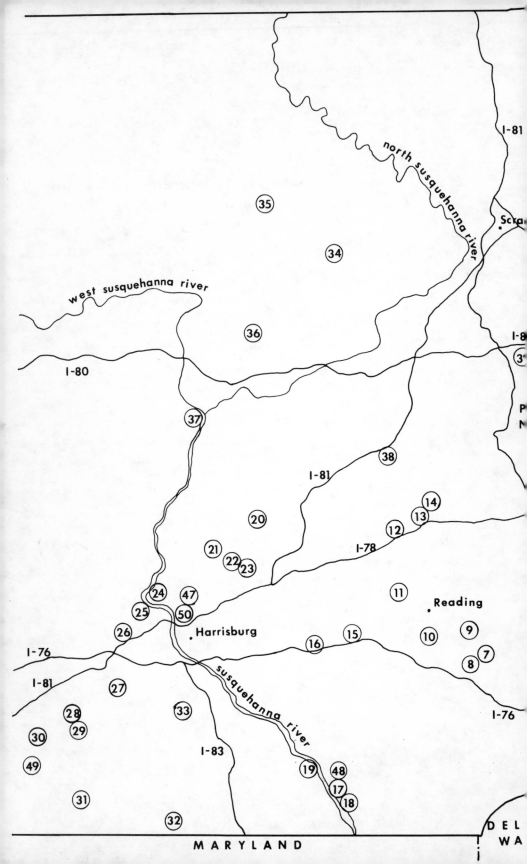

Contents

Introduction 9

Susquehanna West

Northern Tier and
the Pocono Plateau

Backpacks

Introduction

Anyone who likes going out the front door can find a place to explore in eastern Pennsylvania. The mountains, woods, swamps, rivers, fields, hills, and lakes of the part of Pennsylvania roughly defined by the Susquehanna and Delaware rivers, are here represented by fifty hikes grouped into four geographical sections, including one section of backpacking trips. Experienced hikers will feel challenged by many of the hikes in this guide, but trails suitable for the first-time hiker can also delight the mountaineer if the joy of discovery has remained more important than covering more miles a day than anyone else.

This guidebook also covers some unusual places to hike: battlefields, historic areas, bushwhacks around lakeshores, reclaimed strip mines, and a canal towpath to name a few. If you don't have any established hiking trails near you, look for snowmobile paths. In summer they make excellent hiking since they're usually wide, grassy, and free of rocks. Power-line cuts can lead back into the deepest mountains. Or try bush-whacking (hiking cross-country without trails), or following a stream.

Eastern Pennsylvania Trails

These fifty hikes are only a sample of the hikes possible in eastern Pennsylvania. They were chosen for their variety, so you can see what the region has to offer, and to show you that hiking can include more than just remote mountain paths. The hikes are not grouped by difficulty.

Most of the hikes could be called an introduction to the terrain in an area. Other, sometimes longer, hikes nearby

are usually possible if you want to extend your stay in an area. Some of the hikes center around state campgrounds where plenty of public forestland is available for hiking. I've tried to group hikes together so that hikers who are also camping can get in another hike without traveling too far. For example, although Otter Creek (see Hike 19) is geographically in the Susquehanna West section, it is included in the Susquehanna East section because of its driving access and proximity to Kellys Run and Susquehannock State Park (see Hikes 17 and 18). For those who live nearby or are camping in an area, hikes can be lengthened for hikers not so pressed for time.

Perhaps because of its longevity, the Appalachian Trail is what most people think of when asked to name a major hiking trail in eastern Pennsylvania. Indeed, over 140 miles of the AT traverse the eastern part of the state. Yet, not counting the Appalachian Trail, I located over 1,000 miles of hiking trails in eastern Pennsylvania while researching this book. The majority of these trails are on public land: state forests, state parks, and state game lands.

Although not all of these trails are lengthy, a new, major hiking trail, the Pocono Trail, is expected to be 40 to 50 miles in length when completed in 1982. Information and maps of the sections already open are available from the Bureau of Forestry, Department of Environmental Resources, P.O. Box 1467, Harrisburg, PA 17120.

A Pennsylvania trail guide (fall 1980) lists all of Pennsylvania's trails, all major trail clubs, hiking associations, and district forest offices in the state. The guide is available free from the Office of Public Information, Pennsylvania Department of Environmental Resources, P.O. Box 2063, Harrisburg, PA 17120.

If you decide to participate more actively in a hiking club, you can contact the Keystone Trails Association, the name given to an association of over thirty hiking clubs, to find out if a club operates near you: Keystone Trails Association, R.D. 3, Box 261, Cogan Station, PA 17728. The Appalachian Trail Conference is a good source of information about the AT in Pennsylvania, and supplies detailed maps and guidebooks. Write Appalachian Trail Conference, P.O. Box 236, Harpers Ferry, WV 25425.

Total Distance, Hiking Time, and Vertical Rise

The figures for *total distance*, *hiking time*, and *vertical rise* in the heading of each of the fifty hikes are designed to help you decide if a particular hike is suitable for you.

Total distance tells you how far you will hike from start to finish. If mileage for a side trail is not calculated into the total distance, the description will specify. Most hikes are circular, but those that aren't include a return by the same route as part of the total distance. The hikes that are one-way reflect only the distance walked, and include directions for spotting a second car at the end of the hike. Many hikes suggest alternate directions for finishing a hike, and how this would change the total distance.

Vertical rise is the total amount of climbing on a hike. All the climbs are counted, but the figure is not adjusted for elevation lost in descents. For instance, if a hike climbs two mountains, each gaining 500 feet of altitude, the vertical rise for that hike will be 1,000 feet. Generally speaking, the greater the vertical rise per mile, the more challenging the climb. A bushwhack on level

ground might still be a more difficult hike than climbing on a wide, rock-free trail, but the vertical rise is at least some indication of what to expect.

Hiking time is the least precise of hiking guidelines, since it varies with individual pace. The times given calculate only time spent walking. Moving steadily, an average hiker with a day pack on a good trail can cover 2 miles an hour. Don't feel limited by the time given in a hike heading. The purpose of hiking for me has always been to enjoy the outdoors, the walk, and the surroundings.

Maps

Maps listed in hike headings are the United States Geological Survey (USGS) topographical quadrangles for the hike, and any additional state park, historical site, or recreation area maps that would be useful. For this book, sketch maps showing the important turns and side trails on a hike have been prepared on base USGS maps. You won't need maps other than the guide to hike these trails, but the suggested maps provide additional information about geographical features and other hiking trails in an area.

State park maps show all facilities in a state park, but do not show elevation changes or type of terrain—open or forested. They are available at individual state parks or free from the Bureau of State Parks, Department of Environmental Resources, P.O. Box 1467, Harrisburg, PA 17120.

Maps of Pennsylvania's state forests show elevations and all trails but frequently show little detail because the scale can be as small as 1 inch to 3 miles. Since the maps do show all trails and roads in a forest, including nearby state parks, they are useful for planning longer hikes and plotting cross trails. They are available free from the Bureau of Forestry, Department of Environmental Resources,

P.O. Box 1467, Harrisburg, PA 17120.

Maps of individual game lands are available from the Pennsylvania Game Commission, Office of Public Information, P.O. Box 1567, Harrisburg, PA 17120, for a small charge. The maps, however, show few features and are not as reliable for hiking trails as other maps. K.T.A. and P.A.T.C. maps listed in hike headings are maps produced from USGS base maps by the Keystone Trails Association and the Potomac Appalachian Trail Conference.

In many respects, USGS topographical maps are the best maps for hikers. They show mountains, swamps, creeks, lakes, forest cover, elevation change, trails, roads, driveways, buildings—nearly every feature of the land. For hikers, the best scale is the 7½ minute series, 2.5 inches to 1 mile. At that scale, every stream, house, and bend of the trail is visible on the map, making them very easy to follow with only a little practice. USGS maps also come in a 15 minute series, 1 inch to 1 mile. Any map with a scale smaller than 1 inch to 1 mile is of limited use to the foot traveler.

If you're using USGS maps for the first time, you'll find many of the symbols self-explanatory: creeks are blue lines, swamps are small green clumps of grass, houses are black squares, and orchards are small green circles in lines and rows. A green background on the map means that area is forested. A white background denotes open fields. Brown lines show elevation changes plotted every 20 feet and numbered every 100 feet. The closer together the brown lines, the steeper the hills and valleys. Very few brown lines, spaced a quarter of an inch apart or further, show very little elevation change. The tops of mountains are usually shown as exact elevations. A trail is a dotted line, two dotted lines running parallel are usually a woods road. A single dotted line crossing a compacted series of brown lines shows a very severe ascent or descent.

A good way to familiarize yourself with USGS maps is to buy one that includes your home or an outdoor recreation area you know very well, and spend an afternoon locating sites on the map. USGS maps, as well as a state directory listing all USGS maps in Pennsylvania and a guide to map symbols, can be ordered directly from the United States Geological Survey, 1200 Eads Street, Arlington, VA 22202. Backpacking stores often sell USGS quadrangles, and many college libraries have a set of maps available for photo-copying.

You should realize, however, that although USGS maps are constantly updated, new man-made features can obliterate or change natural features. Hiking trails are especially vulnerable to logging, fire damage, disuse, and erosion—conditions that could significantly change what you find from the description or sketch map of a hike.

Clothing and Equipment

First and foremost, you shouldn't set foot on a mountain trail without a decent pair of boots. Pennsylvania has long been known as the rockiest state along the entire Appalachian Trail, and only a comfortable pair of boots will help you negotiate those rocks. Try on boots in the store with the socks you will wear hiking, and don't buy boots that don't feel comfortable. Hiking boots can be a half size longer and wider than street shoes. Waterproof your boots before you head out to the woods and repeat whenever your boots take a soaking. Hike around your house or near home in new boots before venturing onto a trail—it often takes thirty to fifty miles to break in a new pair of boots.

Two pairs of hiking socks with boots are preferable: a light pair of wool socks next to the foot, and a heavy pair of wool socks over these. Wool is more comfortable, longer lasting, and helps repel sweat better than any other material.

Hiking clothing depends largely on the weather you encounter. In summer, a morning or afternoon's walk on a well-worn trail near civilization will require only a light shirt, lightweight, preferably long pants, and a hat or sun visor. For a daylong hike in more rugged territory in the same weather, add a windbreaker or heavier shirt and a bandanna to your day pack. July and August in Pennsylvania can sometimes be too hot to hike during mid-day. Plan your hikes for early morning and evening, or wait for cooler weather. Nothing can ruin a hike faster than heat and exhaustion.

Spring and fall are usually the most pleasurable times for hiking in Pennsylvania. Long pants of heavy cotton, a light T-shirt with a flannel shirt, and a light jacket in your pack will keep you comfortable in most situations. Temperatures in these seasons can change rapidly, especially on top of a mountain, so keep a warm hat and pair of gloves in your day pack. In spring, always take an extra set of socks. Spring rains swell small streams, and getting wet feet on a spring hike is a real possibility. If your feet get wet, put on dry socks immediately—even if your boots are wet, too.

Hiking in cold weather requires a very different kind of dressing. Layers of long underwear, heavy socks, wool shirt, sweater, jacket, and a mountain jacket are needed in the coldest weather. Extra socks and heavy mittens and hats are necessities. Hiking in winter can be great fun; you'll see wider vistas, meet fewer people, and discover that a familiar trail looks completely different under a layer of snow. It is also the most difficult season to hike in and should not be attempted by the inexperienced.

On almost every day hike you should carry a lightweight day pack large enough to hold a jacket, gloves or mittens (seasonal), a canteen of water, a bar or two of nonmelting candy, snacks or a lunch. If I'm only going out for a day I don't bother with cooking equipment, although in winter I might take a can of soup and a heating tablet. A small first-aid kit of band-aids, moleskin for blisters, a snakebite kit, a few aspirin, gauze tape, and matches all fits into a standard-sized band-aid tin. Other items to include in a day pack are insect repellent (seasonal), a compass (not often necessary but a good precaution), hiking maps or trail guide, camera, notepad, and wildlife guides for birds, wildflowers, shrubs and trees. If there's any chance of rain take along a lightweight rain jacket. In most seasons in Pennsylvania you won't need full rain gear on a day hike.

The water you find in eastern Pennsylvania's streams is generally safe to drink if it's running over rocks or sand, but you're better off taking your own water.

Backpacking

You'll need additional equipment if you decide to extend your hiking overnight. The backpack itself shouldn't weigh more than three pounds and should be comfortable when you put it on. Get a store employee to put about twenty-five pounds of something in the pack to see how it feels loaded.

The next important item is a sleeping bag, preferably mummy shape, made of either down or polyfiber. A good sleeping bag should roll up into its own very small stuff bag, and should be rated for its lowest comfortable sleeping temperature. A summer bag shouldn't weigh more than three to four pounds and a winter bag probably not more than five. Under the bag you'll use a foam sleeping mat.

Your next major purchase will be a tent. If you plan to camp only in summer for a short time, a one-person tent big enough only for a sleeping bag may be adequate. If you're planning occasional longer trips, however, a tent you can sit up in might be more comfortable. A summer weight

two-person tent weighs about five to seven pounds, and a winter weight tent weighs slightly more. A backpacking tent should have a rain fly that fits over the top of the main tent to deflect rain.

I never carry much cooking equipment, even when I'm traveling long distance: a small gasoline stove; a two-cup pot; a small, folding fry pan; a sierra cup; and a spoon. A Swiss-army knife also has a can opener, among many other more useless things.

So-called backpacking foods are expensive and unnecessary. Careful supermarket shopping will produce a variety of foods that need only boiling water to prepare. Instant rice, instant soups and stews, jellos, powdered eggs, pancake and biscuit mixes are the basis of my dinners. Vegetables like carrots and celery pack very well if wrapped and placed in the center of the pack. Hard cheese will last for four to five days even in the hottest weather if wrapped in foil and placed in the center of the pack.

Safety

Safeguarding yourself in the woods is pretty much a matter of common sense, even if you're not a veteran woodsman.

Pennsylvania's state game lands and some forest lands are open to hunters during various fall and spring hunting seasons. On established trails, you won't have much problem with hunters, but on the first day of small game and deer seasons, it's best to avoid hiking altogether. Some hikers tie a blaze-orange triangle—such as those used on slow-moving vehicles—to the back of their packs. Hunting is prohibited on Sundays, and the law is enforced.

When you hike, let someone at home know exactly where you're going and when you expect to get back—by leaving a map and itinerary. If there is an accident, someone will search for you. Hiking alone

is not recommended even for an experienced hiker, although you can probably get by safely on a short walk on a well-used trail. If you do hike alone, it's even more important to leave a detailed itinerary at your house and also in your car parked at the trailhead. Tell the ranger on duty at a state park or campground where you're going, and sign in and out on the register of hikers if one is available.

The only potential wildlife problem will be poisonous snakes. Rattlesnakes and copperheads both live in Pennsylvania's mountains. Learn what both snakes look like, and how to identify them. You will see many more nonpoisonous snakes than poisonous ones while hiking, but these are not dangerous unless you tease them. High boots, long pants, and a walking stick are wise precautions.

Hikers should also be aware that a mother bear with cubs can be dangerous, especially in early spring when the sows are just bringing their new youngsters out of hiding. Bear signs in an area are usually hard to miss: bear claw marks on trees remain as scars, alerting you that this is bear country. Many hikers carry "bear bells" on their packs, giving bears time to turn and run when they hear hikers coming.

Respecting the Land and Its Inhabitants

Hiking one spring on a major trail in eastern Pennsylvania I came to a section that was deeply rutted in the forest floor. Hikers, thinking the trail was too rutted, had created a new path next to the original one, now also deeply rutted. Altogether, there were three deep ruts in the trail, and a fourth rut just beginning—a clear example of a grossly overused trail.

Hikers overusing that trail probably didn't think they were damaging the forest, and that's part of the problem. There is an old hiker's saying, "Take only pictures, leave only footprints." I think we've left our footprints for too long in some places, and it's time to rethink that old saw.

A simple way to avoid trail overuse is for hikers to take a more active role in finding their own places to hike. There are many trails in eastern Pennsylvania other than the Appalachian and Horseshoe trails. And there are many more miles of interesting places to safely hike, observe, and explore the outdoors than just on trails. When you do hike on trails, understanding that the land and its inhabitants are fragile is the first step toward respecting both.

Hiking the trails for this book I saw even more animals than when I hiked the entire North Country Trail from New York to North Dakota in 1978, fourteen miles a day for eight months. If you are interested in animals and birds, hike quietly and in a small group. To see the rare lady's-slipper or find the small trailing arbutus, you have to walk slowly, because the plants aren't in the middle of the trail. Joy and discovery in the outdoors—not feats of time and distance—should be the hiker's goal. In the outdoors you must discover the surroundings for yourself. I hope this guide helps you in that discovery.

Legend

_____	trail
. . . .	side trail
P	parking
(P)	alternate parking
AT	Appalachian Trail

Schuylkill
Valley

1

Tyler Arboretum

Total distance: 3.5 miles
Hiking time: 2 hours
Vertical rise: minimal
Maps: USGS 7½' Media; arboretum map

John J. Tyler Arboretum near Philadelphia in Delaware County is a lush 700-acre outdoor greenhouse ideal for wandering. Twenty miles of trails crisscross woods of conifers, oaks, hybrid rhododendrons, and flowering dogwood.

The land comprising the modern arboretum was given to Thomas Minshall by William Penn in 1681, and bequeathed to succeeding generations of Minshalls, Painters, and Tylers. Between 1830 and 1875 the Quaker brothers Minshall and Jacob Painter planted nearly 1,000 trees and shrubs, many imported from around the world. Today, many trees are identified by markers, encouraging visitors to leave the trail and explore. This guide describes only one of many possible meandering paths through the arboretum.

From Philadelphia, follow US 1 southwest to PA 352. Turn right (north). Just beyond Lima turn right again onto Barren Road. Continue less than 1 mile to Painter Road, turn left, and drive northwest past the arboretum on your right. In .5 mile you will reach the entrance and park on the south side of the lot near the main buildings. You can also take US 3 west from Philadelphia to PA 352, 5 miles west of Edgmont. Turn south onto PA 352, and drive 5 miles, 1.5 miles beyond Gradyville. Turn left onto Forge Road, drive .5 mile to Painter Road, and turn right. The entrance to the arboretum is .25 mile on the left.

From the west, take the Pennsylvania Turnpike (I-76) to Downingtown exit 23 where you join PA 100 south. In 3 miles, leave PA 100 for US 202. In another 3 miles, turn left (east) and drive 3 miles to PA 352. Turn right (south), drive 5 miles to Forge Road on the left, and reach Painter Road in .5 mile. Turn right and continue .25 mile to the arboretum entrance.

Once you've arrived at the arboretum, walk south from the parking lot to the barn (arboretum office) for a free map. The arboretum opens at dawn—to accommodate birders—and closes at 5 P.M. in winter and 8 P.M. in summer. East of the barn on the left is Lachford Hall, built in 1738. West of the barn is a Fragrant Garden of flowers and shrubs with markers labeled in braille.

Descend a gentle slope into the parklike Old Arboretum. The massive Cedar of Lebanon, 15 feet in circumference, dominates the other exotic trees here. Cypress, Japanese spruce, cryptomeria, and the small mature Franklin tree, unknown in the wild, are

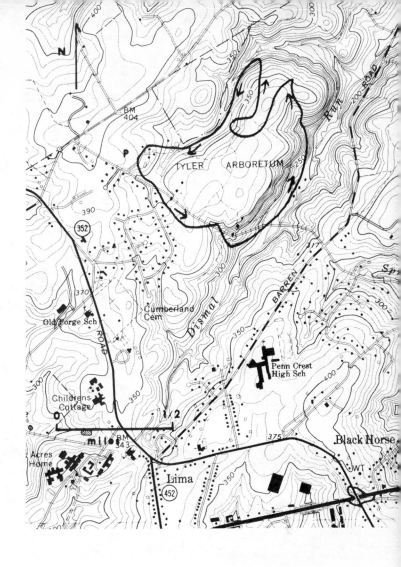

planted about the grassy lawn.

Leave the Old Arboretum and begin your search for the Giant Sequoia. Along the walkway through the Old Arboretum find the red-blazed Painter Brothers Trail and cross a stream. To your left and ahead is the 25-acre Pinetum where pines, spruces, hemlocks, cedars, and other conifers grow. The trail is a broad swath cut through tall grass between the widely-spaced trees. Here long pants would protect you against ticks.

Take time to notice the sounds around you. Many birds, including shyer species chased away by city sounds, nest and find refuge here. Bring a good field guide to birds—and someone who knows bird calls, if you can. I heard the distinctive call of the black-billed cuckoo, "cu cu cu".

Continue on the Painter Trail, bypassing the green-blazed Pinetum Trail to the left. In .5 mile reach the Giant Sequoia on your right. Planted between 1856 and 1860, this 65-foot tree with its towering conical shape is an impressive landmark. To the right, the Pink Hill Trail leads across Painter Road into the South Farm and Pink Hill areas. In late April, flowering mountain pinks carpet the ground where the soil is too barren to support large trees.

Stay on the Painter Trail, leaving the Pinetum plantation. At .6 mile, continue straight ahead where the Painter Trail turns left. At .75 mile turn left onto the orange-blazed Dismal Run Trail, through natural woods where giant monkey vines, ferns, violets, mayapples, and wild ginger abound. If you are hiking with children, urge them to walk quietly to increase your chances of seeing wildlife.

When Dismal Run Trail descends toward the stream at the bottom, at 1.2 miles, you can follow it for a 1-mile loop through the East Woods and a demonstration of active forest management for wildlife, timber, and enjoyment. Or, take one of the paths to the left, east of the Pinetum through an area of spring wildflowers and warblers.

Walking north, at 1.7 miles you run into the yellow-blazed Dogwood Trail; head west through several acres of flowering dogwood. Near the Pinetum (at 2.25 miles), turn right again and enter five acres of rhododendron hybrids—large shrubs with evergreen leaves. In the wild, rhododendron flowers are usually white, or white tinged with faint pink. The colors of these hybrid blooms in early May are strong and vivid—shades ranging from white to orange and red. Photographers find this spot a delight, and I watched an artist with his easel recording the brilliance of the plantings.

Beyond the rhododendron head northeast on any of several trails, past plantings of holly and many-colored azalea. Reach the blue-blazed Rocky Run Trail at 2.3 miles. Turn right, away from the park entrance, into woods of mature oaks and pines, many not native to eastern Pennsylvania.

At 2.5 miles, the Rocky Run Trail loops back west to the arboretum entrance. An open field here provides the steepest climb of the walk. Pass two ponds on the right, cross a tributary of Rocky Run, and at 3.4 miles, reach the east side of the Old Arboretum. Walk north past Lachfield Hall to enter the North Woods. On the left huge collections of ornamental flowering cherry and crabapple, magnolias, daffodils, and lilacs astonish visitors every April and May. The parking lot is just west, to the left. Check for ticks when you reach your car.

Ridley Creek

Total distance: 4.9 miles
Hiking time: 2 hours
Vertical rise: 250 feet
Maps: USGS 7½' Media; state park map

This hike in Ridley Creek State Park just outside Philadelphia offers formal gardens, hardwood forest, a pine plantation, and rolling hills of abandoned farmland beginning to reforest. This Delaware County park 3 miles northwest of Media has become so popular since it opened in 1972 that park officials sometimes close the gates to prevent overcrowding. In early spring and on weekdays, however, you'll find the hiking trails all but deserted.

From Philadelphia, take PA 3 west or US 1 southwest to where it intersects PA 3. Continue on PA 3 to the park entrance, 2 miles west of Newtown Square. From the west, take US 30 east to US 202, turn south, and drive 5 miles to PA 3. Turn left (east) and continue 5 miles to the park entrance.

Turn south on the park road (Sandy Flash Drive North) and drive 2 miles. Turn right on Gradyville Road, then left in .5 mile on Sandy Flash Drive South. In another .5 mile on the right, you'll reach the park office, originally the Hunting Hill Mansion—built in 1914 around a 1789 Pennsylvania stone farmhouse. Turn right to park in the lot east of the mansion.

Begin your hike by exploring the formal gardens west of the mansion. Here you'll find beautiful pools, fountains, and symmetrical plantings. Walk south down a few steps, cross the lawn, and go down a few more steps to the stream near a small pond on the right. Across the bridge a narrow unmarked trail leads through a muddy area of Jack-in-the-pulpits and skunk cabbage. The trail dries out as you walk, ending on Sycamore Mills Road at .4 mile.

Turn left onto Sycamore Mills Road, now used for bicycling, and continue east 200 yards to the White Trail. Turn right, following the white blazes south. (Several trails converge in this section, so watch the blazes carefully.) Walk uphill gradually through mature oaks into an abandoned field now starting to reforest. Because abandoned fields are the main feature of this hike, you'll see more farmlands birds and animals than woodlands wildlife—I saw thrushes and several varieties of warblers in the first mile of hiking. Listen for the whistle of the black-billed cuckoo—three short whistles, a pause, then three more whistles.

At 1 mile cross Sandy Flash Drive South and head uphill past bracken and Christmas ferns beneath oaks and hickories. As you reach a rise, the trail

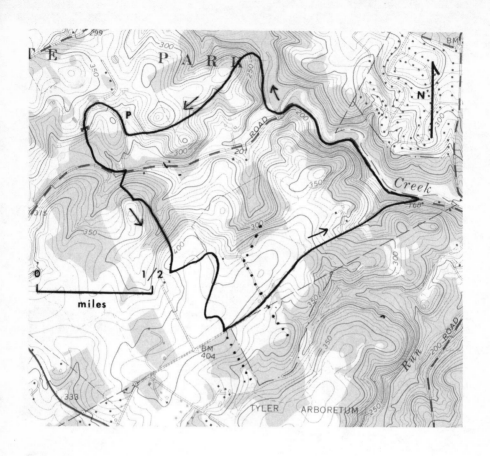

skirts the edge of the woods to open views to the left across rolling overgrown fields. Here reforestation is just getting started. The fields are filled with brambly patches of multiflora rose, 4 to 5 feet tall and 8 to 10 feet across. The plant is a terrible nuisance to eradicate from a field or fence row where it chokes out more desirable crop plants. But it is sought after by small birds that love to hide among the thorns—and by smart birdwatchers. In May the small, pinkish-white flowers fill an entire field with their beauty and sweet fragrance. Around the edge of a field, the trail now turns sharply left, heading northeast through a field dotted with clumps of the multiflora rose.

At 1.4 miles you cross another paved road and picnic area, and then move downhill. Soon you'll reach a trail fork where the Blue Trail branches off to the left. Bear right onto the White Trail, arcing south again. In less than .1 mile, the Red Trail heads off left; continue straight ahead on the White Trail and cross another paved road. Just beyond, the

White Trail parallels an old water run built to channel water through the fields, and reaches a paved bicycle road at 1.9 miles.

Turn left (northeast) downhill and continue 1 mile to Ridley Creek, passing a large pine plantation on the right. Here at the intersection stand several eighteenth-century buildings (now private residences) that were part of an early mill site called Bishops Mills and Upper Providence Corn Mill, in the area now known as Sycamore Mills. Turn left at this intersection to follow the road, which has been closed to vehicles.

Follow Ridley Creek northwest upstream .7 mile beyond Sycamore Mills. Leaving the road at 3.6 miles, turn right onto the Blue Trail .1 mile beyond the second sharp bend to the left (west). The Blue Trail follows the creek, passing an American Youth Hostel on the left. (An easier way to reach the hostel, open year-round, is to continue on the bicycle road for .25 mile, instead of turning onto the Blue Trail.) In .4 mile, the trail swings left and ends in a parking lot at 4.2 miles.

Continue walking southwest downhill across both areas of the parking lot and cross the road into the bicycle rental area to reach a group of planted pines. It doesn't really matter which one of several unmarked trails here you take, if you keep to the southwest and downhill. In 150 yards you leave the pines to enter a large open field covered with multiflora rose and small trees. Wandering here, I followed an old field trail through the rolling hills. In a small vale between two bare hills I stopped to watch white-throated sparrows catch insects in midair and carry them back to their nests in the multiflora rose. Though surrounded by picnic tables just out of view, this small area seems cut off—an excellent place to observe wildlife. I also saw a single deer and several hawks.

If you've found the old two-track then follow it as it winds west through the field. If you haven't, continue west between the two hills, and in .25 mile reach Sandy Flash Drive South. Turn right (north) and follow the road .2 mile to the park office on the left, and your waiting car.

Springfield Trail

Total Distance: 4.5 miles
Hiking time: 2 hours
Vertical rise: 200 feet
Map: USGS 7½' Lansdowne

The Springfield Trail in suburban Philadelphia, maintained by the Springfield Trail Club, shows that a good idea, hard work, and public and private cooperation produce good results. The first hike was in 1969, four years after permission was granted by Springfield Township officials and private owners to cross township parks and private lands. Although the route crosses a suburban housing development, you'll forget you're on the fringes of Philadelphia as you walk along wooded paths residents say were first walked by Indians, and along Crum Creek—an area that observant rock-hounds will find rich in garnets.

To reach this Delaware County trail, take US 1 (City Line Road) southwest out of Philadelphia to PA 320. Turn left (south); in 1 mile turn left again on PA 420 (Woodland Avenue). Park just beyond the intersection on the left (or .6 mile further down PA 420 on the right).

Begin walking southeast on PA 420. In .2 mile turn right onto James Lane, just behind Kovacs Funeral Home. Follow the lane uphill, turn left, and then proceed downhill—off the paved road away from the houses—into the Whiskey Run valley on the Springfield Trail. The pale yellow blazes lead you south along the narrow

Whiskey Run through Spring Valley Park, a local township park. You'll reach Richardson Middle School at .75 mile. The stream valley hides all but an occasional view of nearby houses and businesses, and the forested stream-banks are thick with honeysuckle and other vines.

Local children often come exploring here with friends and dogs. A few look for garnets, but crayfish in the stream seem to be the major attraction. Though children make the trip easily in sneakers, adults with walking shoes instead of hiking boots should use extra caution. The Springfield Trail is an example of good hiking close to people's homes and businesses. This trail provides opportunity to enjoy the outdoors without having to plan a wilderness expedition.

Continue behind Richardson Middle School, and at 1 mile reach the commuter trolley line into Philadelphia. Turn right (southwest), paralleling the tracks. Be sure to stay on the trail and not walk on the tracks. At 1.2 miles cross the trolley tracks and then Thompson Avenue, leaving the tracks to follow a road for about 150 yards, paralleling the tracks at a greater distance. At 1.5 miles cross the tracks again and follow them under the Sproul

Road (PA 320) bridge. At this point, you're about 1 mile north of Swarthmore College, also on PA 320.

Once under the bridge, immediately turn right and follow a short, sharp descent to Whiskey Run. Here, you'll find no evidence of suburban life but only chipmunks, squirrels, and—in the Spring—Jack-in-the-pulpits and violets. At 2 miles you'll cross Paper Mill Road and in .1 mile reach Crum Creek. The trail crosses the creek and turns right (north), leaving the trolley tracks. You can turn right onto Paper Mill Road instead, and walk .5 mile to where the Springfield Trail recrosses Paper Mill Road. Although the trail closely parallels the road, it stays closer to Crum Creek, which has special attractions for the observant hiker.

The land along Crum Creek is rich in silicate minerals. You will easily recognize mica—a transparent, soft, flaky mineral. Feldspar is a dark, streaked mineral often found with mica. If you're very lucky, you may even find garnets —dark red silicate crystals considered to be semiprecious stones. Some are gem quality but others are soft or flawed—more like decayed jewels. I found mica and feldspar along the sandy creek bottom and the rocky sides of the stream, but none of the creek's famous garnets. Since garnets are frequently found with feldspar, any place along the creek might produce a good find.

At 2.7 miles you pass near the remains of an old paper mill. Here, where Crum Creek bends sharply northeast, the trail recrosses the creek, then Paper Mill Road, and heads through Smedley Park and picnic area. Climbing slightly, you come to the most remote section of the hike. Huge hemlocks, over 3 to 4 feet in diameter, grow plentifully amid oaks of

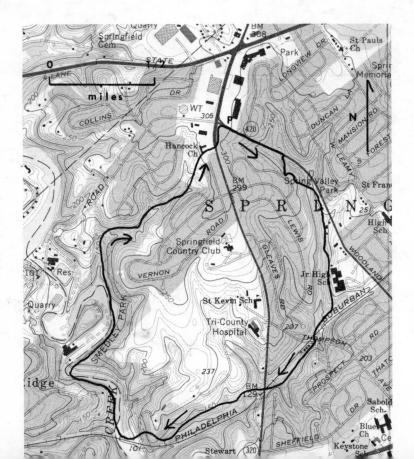

28 *Schuylkill Valley*

nearly equal size, tulip poplars, and sycamores.

The large 100- to 200-year-old trees block the sun here and prevent underbrush growth. In small sunny spots grow clusters of mayapple, wood-sorrel, and wild lily-of-the-valley—a less showy version of the stalks of white bells familiar to gardeners. You may glimpse squirrels, chipmunks, and small garter snakes here, and crayfish and minnows in the stream. Several box turtles calmly retreated to their shells when children approached. Bright orange and gold tree fungus, almost fluorescent in color, grows on some of the fallen hemlocks. You can see down to Crum Creek on your left, but the trail follows the hills above the stream.

At 3.5 miles, the stream narrows and becomes a tributary of Crum Creek. To the right .1 mile is Lownes Park, a playground where swings and basketball courts attract neighborhood youngsters. The children sometimes make their own trails in this part of the woods, so watch the yellow blazes to avoid ending up in a homemade treehouse. Where the stream narrows, the trail is frequently rocky, wet, and slippery. The hills close in on the trail leaving little walking room, and a downed log covered with honeysuckle can force you up the hill on a brief but tricky detour.

After 4 miles you reach a bridge on the right leading to Lownes Park. To complete the Springfield Trail loop, stay with the yellow blazes along the stream until you come out of the woods at Hancock Church. Turn left on PA 320 and continue .1 mile to PA 420. At the intersection turn right on PA 420 to reach your car.

Wissahickon Gorge

Total distance: 4.7 miles
Hiking time: 2½ hours
Vertical rise: 100 feet
Map: USGS 7½' Germantown

Trout and nesting Canada geese are a few of the surprises you'll find hiking through this hemlock- and boulder-filled gorge in Wissahickon Park within the city limits of Philadelphia. The entire Wissahickon Gorge Trail runs 6 miles from near Chestnut Hill College on PA 422, down Wissahickon Creek to its confluence with the Schuylkill just north of US 1. This circuit hike links a bridle trail on the west side of the creek with a return on the Wissahickon Gorge Trail on the opposite bank.

To reach Wissahickon Park from the north, follow US 422 (the Germantown Pike—east of the gorge) south from Montgomery County into Philadelphia County. Or drive south on Ridge Avenue, west of the gorge. From Ridge Avenue turn left onto Bells Mill Road .2 mile after entering Philadelphia County, and continue 1 mile to a parking area on the right. From US 422 turn right onto Bells Mill Road .5 mile after you enter Philadelphia County, just past Chestnut Hill College. Continue .4 mile to the parking lot; both lots on Bells Mill Road are within 100 yards of the trailhead.

Begin on the bridle trail at the bottom of the hill. This is a wide, flat dirt road, now closed to traffic, along the west streambank. You'll be walking among horseback riders, joggers, and mothers with babies in strollers as you head south. In places you can leave the bridle trail to follow a narrow fisherman's path on the left along the very edge of the creek. To your right is a sheer ridge of rocks and hemlocks rising 90 feet. Boston and bracken ferns grow from tiny chinks between moss-covered rocks; chipmunks and squirrels live in rock crevices or among the roots of old trees. In places worn paths lead up the rocks, paralleling the low, rocky ridge or returning to the developed area less than 1 mile uphill.

In .5 mile you reach a picnic area left of the bridle trail. Here I left the trail to walk along the stream where I saw several families picnicking, and among them, a family of a different sort. A pair of Canada geese were showing off their two newly-hatched goslings, only a day or two old and completely covered with grey down. Canada geese are extremely protective of their young; you usually can't get within 50 feet of a brood before the gander prepares to attack. The males are fierce and can easily break the arm of an

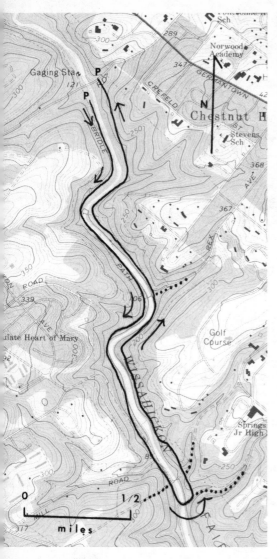

enormous amounts of landmoving—an unlikely prospect for early city builders when land was plentiful. The gorge remained an undeveloped natural area and today covers 3,000 acres in the Fairmount Park system. City noises do not intrude here on the sounds of squirrels, birds, and horses hooves. Above the cliffs are hemlocks, and your return trail.

Beyond the picnic area you come to a wooden covered bridge. Ten bridges cross the Wissahickon along the 6-mile gorge trail, so you can make your hike as long or as short as you like. Walk to the middle of the bridge for a good view of the creek; a small dam just before the bridge offers another good view in both directions.

The bridle trail winds along the creek where fishermen search for trout, wading into the clear cold water, usually not deeper than 3 feet except on the bends. At 1 mile reach a stone bridge boasting arches and stairs at either end. At 2 miles pass another bridge, and less than .1 mile beyond, a fourth bridge. Turn left here across the bridge, and left again upstream, following the red-orange blazes of the Wissahickon Gorge Trail.

The Wissahickon Gorge Trail is like a mountain path—rocky, hilly, narrow, and light years from the wide, flat bridle trail on the other side. Sometimes you are high above the gorge, other times beside it on a grassy path lined with violets, Jack-in-the-pulpits, and trillium. Large hemlocks lie across the trail, and horse tracks are occasionally visible.

At 2.3 miles pass the third bridge again. To the left is Wigard Avenue, and to the right the path leads toward a golf course. The trail clambers up and down over rocks, high above the stream. Good boots are necessary, and extra caution is needed after rain when the rocks are slippery. Large yellow wood-sorrel blooms here, with flowers up to 1 inch and leaves edged with purple. A smaller

adult. These geese, however, allowed quiet visitors to approach within 20 feet before the gander became anxious.

Across a bend in the stream is a 40-foot cliff, absolutely sheer rock worn by water to polished shades of red and tan. Development of narrow, rock-filled Wissahickon Gorge would have required yellow wood-sorrel grows in most of eastern Pennsylvania, but the large variety, which needs a somewhat warmer climate, is not as widespread.

At 3.3 miles reach the stone bridge again. Pass under the stone archway, across a dirt road (Rex Avenue is to the right), under another narrow arch, and climb a series of stone steps. The steps—more like the ascent from a catacomb than a hiking trail—end at the top of the rise, and the narrow trail continues as before.

You soon reach a wide band of boulders high above on the right. Among these rocks, almost a part of the natural outcropping, a rock statue of an Indian looks west beyond the stream. Most visible in winter, the larger-than-life figure crouches among the rocks and may escape notice in the fullness of summer.

From here to the end of the trail, other trails cross the Wissahickon Gorge Trail. Most are short loops that parallel and eventually rejoin the main trail. At 4 miles pass the covered bridge again and at 4.6 miles reach Bells Mill Road. Your car is in the parking area straight ahead, or .1 mile to the left on the other side of the bridge.

Valley Forge

Total distance: 3.8 miles
Hiking time: 2 hours
Vertical rise: 120 feet
Maps: 7½' Valley Forge; state park map

In winter the gentle rolling hills of Valley Forge State Park northwest of Philadelphia must look much as they did when Gen. George Washington's troops camped here during the hard winter of 1777-78. Valley Forge is famous for its role in the development of our nation, but it is not often sought out by hikers. Exploring this important historic site on foot gives you a deeper understanding of the plight of the 3,000 soldiers who died here during that Revolutionary winter. Cross-country skiing this route could further increase your appreciation of Valley Forge, but it is beautiful and haunting in any season.

From Philadelphia or from the west, take the Pennsylvania Turnpike (I-76) to exit 24 at Valley Forge. Drive north on PA 363 for 1 mile, then west on Outer Line Drive past the park office and reception area on the left. In 1 mile, Outer Line Drive reaches the National Memorial Arch. Turn right (northwest) on Gulph Road and right again in .2 mile of County Line Road. In another .25 mile, turn left on Quarry Road and drive .1 mile, just past an equipment workshop. Park at the end of the road.

From Allentown take the Northeast Extension of the Pennsylvania Turnpike (PA 9) south to its intersection with I-276, just north of Philadelphia. Head west on

I-276 to Valley Forge, exit 24, and follow the rest of the driving instructions.

This circuit hike begins and ends in the rolling, tall-grass field called the Grand Parade. The footing is easy and well suited for a family outing. Avoid the dirt road ahead of you for now; it will be your return route. Walk to your left (northwest) skirting the edge of the woods, left, and the Grand Parade on your right. Although there are no trails, the Grand Parade is excellent for hiking and solitude: no roads or traffic cross the field, and few visitors to Valley Forge explore places without roads or trails. Washington's men drilled on the Grand Parade under Baron Friedrich von Steuben, who attempted to instill some discipline and military awareness into the ragamuffin troops.

Due west .5 mile is Baptist Road. Instead of heading toward the road, go along the edge of the field to a nursery of planted seedlings. Once past the young trees at .3 mile, turn north into the field. The tall grass hides holes, stones, and ticks—in spring and early summer wear long pants for protection.

At 1 mile arrive at PA 23, which crosses Valley Forge State Park. If you turned north before reaching Baptist Road you should reach the highway right at Star Redoubt, a grass-covered star-shaped mound of earth visible before you reach PA 23. The points of this small (50 feet across, 15 feet high) battlement once commanded views north to the Schuylkill. Cross PA 23 to visit Star Redoubt. Then head left (west) on the sidewalk along PA 23. In .4 mile turn onto the first road to the right. Where the road curves left in .1 mile, a trail bears right downhill towards the Schuylkill, at 1.5 miles. Turn right into the woods on the Boundary Trail, soon parallel to a set of railroad tracks.

At 1.6 miles the trail turns sharply right (south) uphill, loops back north, and then east again at 1.8 miles. The dense woods are oak and small white pine, with thick raspberry and honeysuckle underbrush. In spring I saw chickadees, peewees, and many species of migrating spring

warblers: a parula warbler, a pair of black-throated green warblers, besides the more common yellow warbler.

At 1.9 miles you will be opposite an island in the river on your left. Not visible from the trail except in winter, the island was strategically important during Washington's winter encampment—the British could have crossed the Schuylkill here, at the shallows between the west end of the island and the south riverbank called Fatland Ford. Just east of the island is the site of Sullivans Bridge, another potential crossing point. Revolutionary troops observed these two strategic points from Star Redoubt to the south —uphill on your right. If you leave the trail, turn left, and cross the railroad tracks and narrow band of woods, you can see the island.

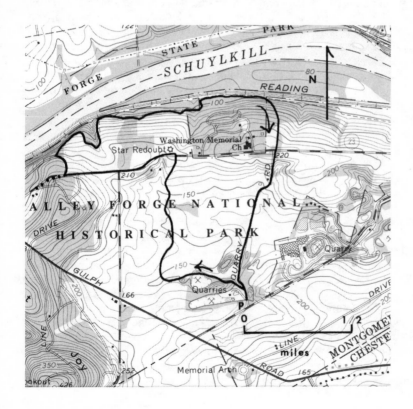

Back on the Boundary Trail, a faint path leads right uphill at 2.5 miles. No landmark marks the spot, but several trails in this vicinity head south and uphill from the Boundary Trail back to PA 23. Turn right, and in .25 miles you'll reach PA 23, heading west or east for a short distance on PA 23, if necessary, to the intersection with Quarry Road.

Cross PA 23 and continue south on historic Quarry Road, the dirt two-track you avoided when you began. Behind and to the right you can still see Star Redoubt overlooking the Grand Parade and the Schuylkill. The position of Valley Forge offered excellent views of both the western approach to the city of Philadelphia and movement along the Schuylkill.

To your right a short way across the Grand Parade, a tall granite obelisk marks the grave of Lt. John Waterman of Rhode Island, the only one of the 3,000 men who died that winter whose identity is known today. Beside the Grand Parade and further south, Washington's cold and starving men were put to work building

their quarters and battlements. Here we find redans, lunettes, and rifle pits. The army moved into Valley Forge in December 1777, but living quarters weren't ready until February. The huts themselves, visible along the roads around Valley Forge, are little more than small, drafty log shacks. In the spring, with the arrival of milder weather, life returned to near-normal in the camp. The British had been kept from attacking Valley Forge and eventually were to withdraw from Philadelphia and Pennsylvania.

At 3.3 miles, pass the headquarters of Jedediah Huntingdon, one of Washington's senior officers. After 1 mile on Quarry Road reach your car. More information on the winter encampment and guides to landmarks are available at the park office, open from 9 A.M. to 5 P.M. daily. No actual battle was fought here, but for many Americans, the winter at Valley Forge has come to symbolize the difficulty of winning independence. That determined struggle is made more alive and real by walking on this ground.

Lehigh Canal Towpath

Total distance: 4.1 miles
Hiking time: 2½ hours
Vertical rise: minimal
Maps: USGS 7½' Easton; park map

Hiking along the Lehigh Canal Towpath in Hugh Moore Park in Easton brings to mind memories of the heyday of canals in the nineteenth century, when mules guided coal-filled barges to Easton and Philadelphia. Part of this canal operated until 1931, and was thus in active use for over 100 years. Today, sections of Lehigh Canal Towpath and the Delaware Canal Towpath are open to hikers and bicyclists, a total of nearly 60 miles of trails from New Hope near Philadelphia to the Easton area.

The section of the Lehigh Canal near Easton, completed in 1978, is considered the epitome of canal restoration. In summer, barges now laden with tourists ply the waters up and down the narrow canal, today a multipurpose recreation site for hikers, fishermen, and picnickers. The Lehigh Coal and Navigation Company began construction of the canal in 1827, two years after the Erie Canal was finished. The two-way waterway was designed to transport anthracite coal from deposits near Mauch Chunk (now called Jim Thorpe) down 46 miles to the Delaware Canal at Easton. To overcome the elevation change of 353 feet, the canal needed fifty-two locks, each 100 feet by 22 feet, and eight dams with slackwater pools. The barges—carrying coal, passengers, or other goods—continued south on the Delaware Canal 60 more miles to metropolitan Philadelphia.

To reach the Glendon area of Easton, take the Twenty-fifth Street exit off US 22 at Easton, about 15 miles east of Allentown. Continue 2 miles south, turning left at the end of Twenty-fifth Street. In .2 mile turn left again at the Hugh Moore Park entrance. Parking is to the right, summer barge rides to the left after you enter the park.

Begin your hike on the River Trail from the north side of the parking lot. The narrow path winds east along the very edge of the river, among waist-high weeds and black raspberries that ripen sometime in June. Bitterberry bushes, plants almost identical to raspberry bushes, with slightly larger leaves and berries covered with fuzzy pods before they ripen, are found here, too. Although the ripe berries look exactly like red raspberries, don't eat them. They're not poisonous but unpalatable, so terribly bitter that you simply have to spit them out.

Along the River Trail are occasional crumbling brick walls and chimneys of the Old Glendon Iron Works, an iron-smelting site in the nineteenth century. The forest through here is dark and oaken, making the ruins between the river and the canal seem eerie even on a sunny day. In spring you'll find Jack-in-the-pulpits, mullein, and yellow evening-primroses along the stream, and scent the sweet perfume of honeysuckle and wild roses in the air.

Along the slow-moving river fishermen mix with canoeists, geese, mallards, and frogs, with placid unconcern. The narrow river gives the mallards little room to escape approaching boaters, so the ducks swim to shore and wait their turn. In a shallow spot at the edge of the river, huddled around a large rock, hundreds of tiny catfish swim as one in a football-sized school.

After 1 mile you'll notice that the hill on your right is actually the high bank of the canal. Small trees and bushes on the bank blend in with the undisturbed land, looking—after 150 years—nearly as natural as one of the oaks along the river. If you climb the bank, you'll find yourself on the towpath overlooking the water. The canal here is 60 feet across at the water line, 45 feet across at the bottom, and 6 feet deep.

Where the river makes a wide bend to the right, you can see small, tree-covered

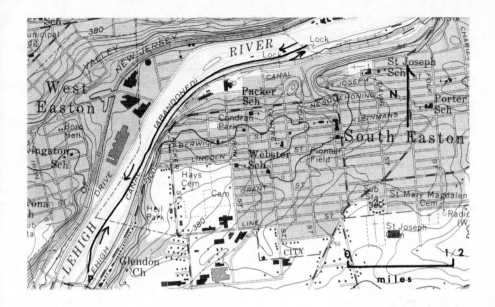

Slag Island Natural Refuge on the left. Hunting and collecting are prohibited on the island, home base for the noisy mallards and geese along the Lehigh. (Bear left on the towpath to reach the Lehigh's confluence with the Delaware River and canal, and the Canal Museum in .7 mile, just across PA 611. The museum is open year-round Tuesday through Friday from 10 A.M. to 4 P.M. and weekends from 1 P.M. to 5 P.M.)

Turn right on the Towpath Trail at Outlet Lock 48 at 2 miles to return to your car. The canal is wide and tree lined, looking more like a sleepy southern river than a man-made canal in Pennsylvania. The flat, rock-free towpath would make a good cross-country ski trip in winter, but a few curves on the River Trail might be difficult to negotiate on skis.

West of Outlet Lock 48 is Lock 47. At the locks the canal narrows into what looks like a concrete and wooden chute. Here a barge once entered the narrow gateway, the gate behind it closed, and water was pumped out of the lock until it reached the depth of the water downstream. The gate ahead then opened, and the barge continued downstream. To go upstream, water was pumped into the lock to raise the water level. Neither lock is used even by the tour barges today, but they seem intact. The heavy, 15-foot wooden gates at one time opened and closed easily; now tree limbs and debris from the canal block the gates, which stand open a few inches to let water through.

At 3.9 miles the canal bends to the left, and at 4 miles an unobtrusive road to the right leads away from the canal back to your car. The road is difficult to spot, and an easier return is to continue until you reach the bridge across the canal at 4.1 miles. Turn right, then right again when you reach the river, to backtrack .1 mile to your car.

7

Hopewell Village and Baptism Creek

Total distance: 5.25 miles
Hiking time: 2½ hours
Vertical rise: 550 feet
Maps: USGS 7½' Elverson; state park map

A walk through Hopewell Village National Historic Site southeast of Reading will take you back in time to a nineteenth-century iron foundry and "company town" in rural Pennsylvania between 1820 and 1840. Beyond the village you'll hike from the Baptism Creek Environmental Study Area to the Chestnut Hill section of French Creek State Park.

French Creek State Park, which surrounds the 5,000-acre Hopewell Village, is 7 miles northeast from the Pennsylvania Turnpike (I-76), exit 22. From the exit, turn right uphill beyond the toll booth; in 1 mile turn right again on Hopewell Road, following signs to French Creek State Park at all turns. At 3 miles pass Jones Millpond on the right, and 1 mile beyond, the road to Geigertown on the left. In 1 mile Hopewell Road becomes Park Road. Continue another 2 miles to the family camping area on the left, and turn right on the paved road by the brick campstore. In .5 mile bear right at a **Y** and reach PA 345 in .5 mile. Turn left, reaching the entrance of Hopewell Village in 1.3 miles. Turn left again and continue .25 mile to the visitor's center and parking lot. You can also reach the village from exit 22 on I-76 by turning right on PA 23 and driving 4 miles to PA 345. Turn left to reach

Hopewell Village on the left in 3 miles.

From Reading or Pottstown, drive US 422 for 7 miles to PA 82, turn south, and cross the Schuylkill into Birdsboro. Turn left on PA 724 and right almost immediately on PA 345, which bisects French Creek State Park, and drive 4.5 miles to the village entrance. Turn right and drive .25 mile to park in the lot. Admission is free, and you can pick up brochures and maps at the visitor's center, open daily from 9 A.M. to 5 P.M.

The Valley Forge-Reading wagon road, dating from 1757, is just below the visitor's center. Cross the road and bear right through the village to an anthracite furnace and a reconstructed charcoal hearth. Remains of similar charcoal pit hearths are visible along the Turtle Trail in French Creek State Park (see Hike 8).

Pass the hearth and bear right, away from the village to Hopewell Lake, dam, and waterfall. Water from the lake was channeled into a race, which flowed into the village where it turned a waterwheel to produce power for the community. Cross the stream at the base of the falls, following the impoundment until you reach the end of a paved park road. Turn sharply left, moving back to the village on a broad trail that ends near tenant houses

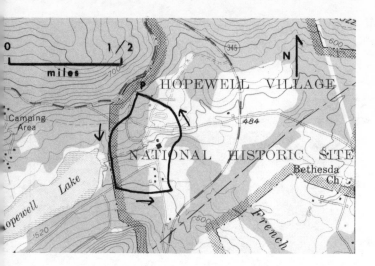

and a boarding house for foundry workers and their families.

To your left is the heart of the complex, isolated from other towns by the need to build a foundry close to the source of iron ore. The main business of the community was the iron foundry: the founder oversaw the furnace, workers labored in twelve-hour shifts without holidays, the noisy waterwheel turned constantly, and the night-and-day operation of the furnace covered the town with charcoal soot. Clement Brooke, the owner, lived in nineteenth-century luxury with a household staff of wives and daughters of furnace workers in his stone "big house" overlooking the village.

Pass the blacksmith shop to reach the casting house where molten iron was ladled into sand molds. Cookware and stoves were the most frequently produced items; by 1844, Hopewell molders had made over 65,000 stoves, many of them the Franklin fireplace type. After 1845 only pig iron was produced, and the iron industry continued to decline until 1883 when the furnace "blew out" for the last time. Inside the casting house the 22-foot

waterwheel turns slowly, its giant wooden frame creaking so loudly it can be heard throughout the village.

Leave the village and walk uphill toward the visitor's center, angling right through the apple orchard to the entrance road. Turn right here at .5 mile, reaching PA 345 in .25 mile. Cross PA 345 and continue straight ahead on the paved road between two fields once worked by foundry workers. In the field to the right, I saw a wild turkey parading like a king, protected from hunters here.

In .25 mile the road curves right across a tributary of Baptism Creek, which runs into French Creek further south. Just before you reach Baptism Creek, head left on a trail into the woods at 1 mile. In 100 yards the path splits; stay left to recross the tributary of Baptism Creek. Beside the path, metal markers point out trees, flowers, and ecosystems—part of the Baptism Creek Environmental Study Area self-guided nature walk.

When the trail splits again, turn left uphill on a rocky unnamed trail. The trail bends right .2 mile beyond a small springhouse, then passes the boulders called Picnic Rock on the right. You soon enter a pine grove and then bear left around a dense thicket of scrub growth where I surprised a large whitetail deer, to top Chestnut Hill at 2.1 miles.

Turn right on the jeep-wide Fire Trail, a flat, rock-free grassy lane that is airy and cool. Pass a trail on the left and cross a power-line cut after .5 mile on the Fire Trail. To the left a short distance is the rocky hillside and a fine view of fields below. (The cut continues southeast down the mountain, reaching the Raccoon Trail along Baptism Creek.) Continue straight ahead and in .25 mile reach another trail intersection marked by a tall, lone hemlock. (The white-blazed trail to the left runs to Millers Point in .75 mile.)

In .5 mile the yellow-blazed Buzzard Trail comes in from the left. Stay on the Fire Trail and head downhill, away from the airy pines atop Chestnut Hill. At 3.3 miles turn right onto the black-blazed Raccoon Trail, descending through a hollow where you'll pass skeletons of chestnut trees killed in the blight that swept through here in the 1930s. In places the Raccoon Trail is narrow and difficult to follow, though the path is usually visible. Make sure you follow the black blazes where the yellow-blazed Buzzard Trail heads off left again.

At 4.2 miles return to the Baptism Creek area and the paved road. Turn left (south, downhill) to retrace your route back to Hopewell Village, where a water fountain in the visitor's center provides relief on a hot day.

44 *Schuylkill Valley*

French Creek State Park

Total distance: 4.75 miles
Hike time: 2½ hours
Vertical rise: 450 feet
Maps: USGS 7½' Elverson; state park map

French Creek State Park 30 miles west of Philadelphia prides itself on variety. It offers sledding, skiing, and ice fishing in winter, 30 miles of hiking trails in 6,800 acres, plus a mixture of northern and southern forest. Most of this hike passes through the northern hardwood forest prevalent in eastern Pennsylvania—oak, hemlock, and hickory. Near the end of the hike, in open areas with southern exposure and protection from harsh winter winds, you'll see southern forest as well. Dogwood, sassafras, pink azalea, and Pennsylvania's state flower, mountain laurel, cover the hills with color in spring and early summer. An excellent trail map is available for fifty cents from the Brandywine Outing Club, Wilmington, DE 19803.

Driving access for French Creek State Park is the same as for Hopewell Village and Baptism Creek (see Hike 7). After entering the park, drive 2 more miles to the campground area and park by the brick camp store.

Across Park Road from the store and luncheonette is the family campground and the trailhead. Begin on the yellow-blazed Horseshoe Trail, which follows the road through the campground. You soon bear left on the trail, following it to the right uphill past large beech trees tatooed with the initials of lovers no longer young. The wide trail is peppered with football-sized ironstone, the kind used in the furnaces of Hopewell Village 2 miles away.

At .5 mile you'll reach a trail intersection and turn left onto the white-blazed Turtle Trail. This is a flat, rock-free path that offers good cross-country skiing in winter. At .7 mile pass the first remains of a half dozen charcoal hearths on the Turtle Trail. Difficult to distinguish now, the hearths are circular depressions in the forest floor, between 30 and 40 feet across. In the nineteenth century great mounds of wood were stacked and burned for two weeks to produce charcoal for the ironworks at Hopewell Village.

At 1.25 miles turn right, following the white blazes. Sometimes thicket obscures the broad forest path for a few feet. In early spring the Turtle Trail is boggy in small low sections where natural springs seep through. In the soggy patches you'll find violets, Jack-in-the-pulpits, and skunk cabbage. The latter looks like garden cabbage and smells decidedly like skunk. The scent is barely noticeable as you walk through the area, but will chase

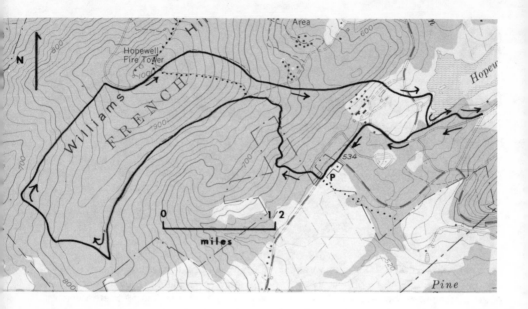

you away if you bruise the leaves or crush the plant.

At 1.75 miles turn again and then make a third right turn in a very swampy area at 2 miles. Leave the Turtle Trail for the Ridge Trail up Williams Hill at 2.3 miles, a right turn well marked with bright red blazes. Climb gradually, ending at 2.75 miles on a paved road. Turn right uphill to a fire tower and picnic area in .3 mile.

At the fire tower many of the park's trails meet or cross, so watch carefully to pick up the right one. Continue along the paved road to the cul-de-sac just beyond the fire tower. Among the picnic tables to the left, the yellow-blazed Horseshoe and blue-blazed Boone trails converge, running concurrently for a few feet before separating at 3.2 miles. Take the left fork, the Boone Trail, northeast downhill off Williams Hill. (To shorten your hike, follow the yellow-blazed Horseshoe Trail southeast back to the campground where you parked.) Shortly you'll pass a group of cabins on the left. At 3.8 miles the trail heads right, off the ridge, and reaches the park maintenance area. Cross the dirt road, leaving the Boone Trail and the white oak woods of the northern forest behind.

Turn left (east) and cross a wide field to Hopewell Lake. The 68-acre lake abounds with Canada geese and mallards during spring and fall migrations, with sizeable colonies that stay year-round. In early April I saw a large flock of migratory coots on the lake, distinguishable by their slate grey bodies, nearly black heads, white bills, and small white spots beneath their tails. Hunting is not permitted in the Hopewell Lake area, and ducks and geese greet each car expectantly for handouts of stale bread or corn.

Walk south of the lake along the access road near the bathing and picnic areas, toward the area called Mount Pleasant. Here the southern forest of flowering trees and shrubs is more in evidence. This area is a transition between the warmer climatic zone of Philadelphia and the colder zone of Reading. Pale pink and white dogwoods, bright pink to white azaleas, and the distinctive red flowers of redbud bring a profusion of color in April and May. These shrubs, though growing wild in French Creek State Park and in the South, will winterkill even in Pottsville and Sunbury, where only the most careful gardener can cultivate them.

Return to the southwest corner of the lake to join the paved road to the park office—or cross the field again to reach the office. Turn left, staying on the road, and in .1 mile you are back at your car.

Daniel Boone Homestead

Total distance: 3 miles
Hiking time: 1 ½ hours
Vertical rise: 40 feet
Maps: USGS 7 ½' Birdsboro; homestead pamphlet

This hike on the Daniel Boone Homestead near Birdsboro in Berks County southeast of Reading takes you through woods and fields where young Daniel, the future frontiersman, learned to hunt, trap, and find his way in the wilderness. The area, no longer remote but still rural, reminds us that mountains aren't the only interesting places to hike. Daniel Boone's birthplace, now a 600-acre Pennsylvania Game Commission sanctuary, is also only a few miles from Hopewell Village and French Creek State Park (see Hikes 7 and 8).

To reach the historic site, take US 422 east from Reading 7 miles to Legislative Route 06107 (LR 06107), just past the right turnoff for Baumstown. Turn left at the intersection, clearly marked to the Daniel Boone Homestead. In 1 mile fork left, also well marked, and continue 1 mile on the twisty, narrow road. Park near the museum on the left. From Philadelphia take US 422 northwest 7 miles beyond Pottstown to LR 06107 on the right; then follow the rest of the driving instructions. If you're staying at French Creek State Park, take PA 345 north 4 miles to PA 724. Turn left and drive to Birdsboro where you join PA 82 north for 1 mile. Turn right in Baumstown on the only road east. In .4 mile turn left (north) on LR 06107, reach US 422 in .2 mile, and

continue ahead on LR 06107, following the rest of the driving directions.

Visitors must pay a small fee for a guided tour of the cabin where Boone was born, but the museum and grounds are free. Visit the museum for exhibits illustrating Boone's life, to orient yourself by the large map of the grounds, and to pick up a free sketch map. Museum hours during months of daylight saving time are 8:30 A.M. to 5 P.M. weekdays, and Sundays, 1 P.M. to 5 P.M. Winter hours are shorter. Telephone the museum before you arrive to make sure the facility is open and for information about demonstrations featured periodically during the summer.

The Daniel Boone Homestead is a good area for wandering; this hike combines a fisherman's path and a bridle trail, and also crosses fields and the Daniel Boone Woods. Outside the museum, head southwest along a fence to the western end of the pasture. Just ahead and slightly right are several small buildings. Turn right at the sawmill, one of the summer historical exhibits, passing a small cemetery on the right.

At .3 mile begin walking around the north side of Daniel Boone Lake on Owatin Creek. The lake has open fishing for bluegills and other warm-water species, but the large numbers of Canada geese that inhabit the lake discourage visitors who get too close. Follow a fisherman's path along the lakeshore and into the woods. At .5 mile you'll reach the headwaters of the lake, where chickweed—a tiny plant with pretty white flowers—covers the forest floor.

At .6 mile the undergrowth of multiflora rose and small saplings is so thick that passage is difficult. Leave the faint trail to head northwest across the open unworked field on the right behind the Boone cabin, visible when you reach the top of the small rise in the rolling field. Daniel Boone was born here in a log house in 1734, four years after his Quaker parents settled the land. The Boone family came to this country sometime before 1713, when it was still sparsely settled and the edge of

the wilderness. When Daniel was 16 his family decided the area was becoming too thickly settled for them. They wanted to find better land, and Daniel's father had not found favor with the local community of Friends Meeting (Quakers). In 1750 they moved to the Yadkin Valley of North Carolina, and Daniel returned to Pennsylvania only a few times in his long life.

Continue northwest through the field of small white pines and multiflora rose. At 1 mile I found a large patch of ripening wild strawberries, and shared them with a box turtle. A short distance beyond the strawberries you'll reach an unmarked bridle trail that crosses the field. Turn right, walking north and then northeast along the bridle trail. Eventually you turn south to skirt the edge of the field.

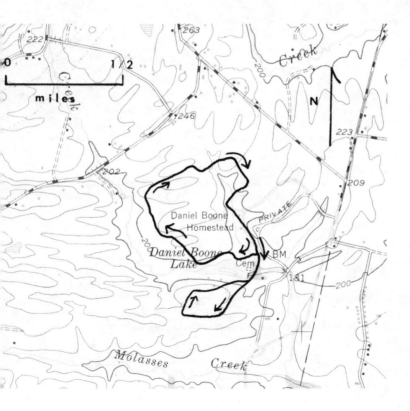

After 1.8 miles, you come to the Bertolet log house, home of another eighteenth-century family. The cabin is boarded up now, but through a crack you can see the huge logs, wide floorboards, and fireplace that reveal the massive size of timber growing here when settlers arrived. At 2 miles the bridle trail passes the Boone homestead on the left. Part of the two-story house was built by Daniel's father, who was a weaver, blacksmith, and farmer. Restoration of the house revealed that the foundation of the Boone cabin formed part of the foundation wall of the present house. At one end, large flat rocks cover the floor of an unfurnished low room—believed to be the foundation and spring of the original cabin.

The bridle trail ends near the Boone house. Head back toward the small museum next door, cross the entrance road, and turn right (south). Instead of bearing right toward the sawmill and cemetery again, continue south into the Daniel Boone Woods, a protected area where you are likely to see quail, pheasants, grouse, rabbits, raccoons, deer, and perhaps a fox. Several trails wind through this tall forest of oak and hickory edged with cedar, but you can easily bushwhack your own loop through the small wooded area free from dense undergrowth and rocks. Molasses Creek, which cuts across to the south .5 mile after you enter the woods, would make a good objective, although this hike doesn't continue that far. Spring wildflowers are abundant in Boone's woods—trillium, spring-beauties, saw-toothed violets, and many others.

Come out of the woods where you entered, just south of the sawmill. The museum should be visible from the edge of the woods; return to your car .25 mile straight ahead.

10

Nolde Forest

Total distance: 5 miles (approximate)
Hiking time: 2 hours
Vertical rise: 300 feet
Maps: USGS 7½' Reading; state park map

This hike in Berks County near Reading is only one of many possible in Pennsylvania's first state park specifically designated for environmental education. Literally crisscrossed with hiking and bridle trails, Nolde Forest's 644 acres were originally owned at the turn of the century by the Jacob Nolde family, who began the extensive forestry and water management of the estate. The renovated Nolde mansion is now a conference center providing offices and classrooms for teachers and students. Hiking in Nolde Forest makes an excellent family outing: you can easily tailor your walking distance to your family's ability, and the many observation blinds and teaching stations offer unique opportunities to learn about nature.

Directions for this hike are more general than others in the guide, concentrating on sights in the park rather than on exact lefts and rights. Exploring off the main trails is easy and encouraged, and you can't get lost in this small area laced with paths. Good walking shoes are adequate although hiking boots are preferable.

Nolde Forest is located on PA 625 about 3 miles south of Kenhorst, a suburb of Reading 1 mile south of the city limits. From east or west take the Pennsylvania

Turnpike (I-76) to exit 21 and turn north on US 222. Where US 222 bears left in 3 miles, turn right and drive 2 miles into Knauers. Here, turn left (north) on PA 625 and head toward Reading until you reach the park entrance in 5 miles. Continue north to park in the bus parking lot near the sawmill. From Lancaster take US 222 northeast 21 miles to the Knauers turnoff; then follow the rest of the driving instructions.

Your hike begins at the bus parking lot, just north of the mansion and main park entrance. Begin walking southwest along Punches Run which winds through the center of the park. Forested hills rise on either side of the tiny stream, full of creatures children love to discover —crayfish and salamanders. The hill on the north side of the run is steeper and wilder than the south hill, which rises to PA 625 and the mansion. From the parking area trails follow both sides of the stream—take your pick.

In .1 mile leave the trail and head south (left) toward the conference center. The brick mansion resembles a miniature old English castle with elaborate windows and doors. Look carefully for handwrought door hinges and iron boot scrapers with nursery themes—a cow jumping over the

52 *Schuylkill Valley*

moon or a dish running off with a spoon.
Outside the house are extensive gardens
and fountains, including a lion head
spouting water into a tiled pond. The
center and library are open daily
until 4 P.M.

Continue along Punches Run southwest
of the conference center to a series of
feeding stations and observation blinds.
Corn, bird feed, or suet are placed along
the creek in cleared areas animals
normally frequent. About 25 feet away
from the feeding stations are tall, wooden
walls with small openings at various
points. These are blinds for watching
wildlife feed. Wild turkey and whitetail
deer are frequent visitors, but the stations also draw raccoons, pheasants,
rabbits, and squirrels. Bird feeders
lure black-capped chickadees, gold
finches, purple finches, indigo buntings,
grosbeaks, and many other flyers.

Leave Punches Run and head left
uphill, past the water tower system that
once supplied fresh water to the Nolde
mansion. Water stored in a tank was
forced downhill by gravity through a pipe
to the house. Soon you reach a pine
plantation. Here stand rows of tall, mature
conifers providing airy walking on even
the hottest days. Trails run to the end of
one row of pines, then return to almost the
same point through the next row, linked by
connector paths between rows. In this
area south of the conference center you
are roughly paralleling PA 625. Surrounding the pine plantation is a stately
forest of red, black, and white oaks.
Hunting is not permitted in any season,
which makes Nolde Forest a delight in the
fall when oak leaves carpet the forest floor
in brilliant patterns.

When you reach the south end of the
park, you'll find a bridle trail. Follow this
path northwesterly along the park
boundary to Punches Run. Deer graze
along the old woods road in this swampy
corner where purple and saw-toothed

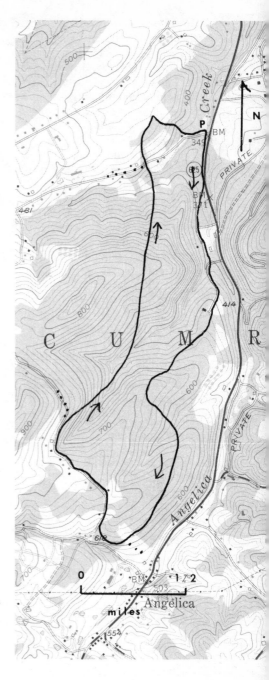

violets, lush ferns, and skunk cabbage edge the path in spring.

Cross Punches Run, leaving the bridle trail to head northeast toward the center of the park. This short uphill section is the most severe climb in the park—not too difficult for the average person, or even young children if you climb slowly and carefully. Head straight uphill through a narrow, rocky hollow for a good view of Punches Run from near the top of the hill. At the top, violets bloom amid heavy boulders in a rocky field. In late summer look for wild asters.

From the hilltop north of Punches Run, all trails including the bridle trail lead northeast toward a small pond at the northern end of the park. You'll probably "hear" the pond a few steps before you head downhill into the watershed of Angelica Creek. Deep-voiced bullfrogs are easily identified among the chorus of many species including smaller, higher-pitched tree frogs. Snakes and snapping turtles haunt the pond, and woodpeckers the trees above. Mosquito repellent is a good addition to your day pack if you tarry awhile to observe the life of the pond.

To return to your car, go southwest back up over the hill and down to Punches Run and the parking lot. Hiking mileage is almost impossible to calculate in Nolde Forest. Trails frequently intersect every 100 yards or so, and confusion about exact trails is likely—losing your way entirely is not. The park itself is a triangle of land bounded by paved roads—Church Road on the north, Oregon Road on the west and south, and PA 625 on the east. In general, heading downhill will bring you to either Punches Run, or Angelica Creek and Church Road. If you can tell direction from the sun, or remember whether you're heading north or south, you won't have any trouble.

11

Blue Marsh Lake

Total distance: 5 miles
Hiking time: 2½ hours
Vertical rise: minimal
Maps: USGS 7½' Bernville; Army Engineers brochure

Blue Marsh Lake near Bernville and Reading is a pretty man-made lake of fingers and inlets frequented mostly by anglers and swimmers since it opened in 1978. Hikers will find the shoreline an interesting route for a bushwhack—hiking without trails. Children will enjoy a short exploration of the lakeshore, while experienced hikers can lengthen a bushwhack into a more strenuous hike. Created by damming Tulpehocken Creek for flood control and water supply in the Delaware Valley Basin, the lake sits in a broad valley populated with more deer, pheasants, and songbirds than people.

Blue Marsh Lake lies 7 miles northwest of Reading along PA 183, southeast of Bernville. Drive PA 183 from Reading to a well-marked left turn just beyond Mount Pleasant to enter the lake area. Continue 1.5 miles toward the beach and concession area to park in the lot near the beach house. From Harrisburg or Allentown take I-78 to PA 183 just north of Strausstown. Drive south on PA 183 for 8 miles (1 mile beyond Bernville) to the entrance road on the right.

The first part of the hike hugs the lakeshore on a narrow angler's path. You then leave the shore to walk through fields and woods with the lake almost constantly in view. You'll be hiking by sight rather than compass on this bushwhack, using obvious landmarks like the fingers of the lake as guides. If you hike in spring or fall, bring a bird guide to identify migrating warblers and waterfowl.

From your car head downhill toward the lake, then west along the shore. Just beyond the beach area you'll reach a stream at .2 mile. A narrow fisherman's path leads upstream 50 feet where you can easily jump across. Continue uphill, dodging low branches and groundhog burrows. Turn left at the edge of a field, walk 25 yards to the end and turn right. In 30 yards turn left on a path downhill back toward the lake, crossing a patch of poison ivy and small hill of thistles with purple flowers the size of chrysanthemums on 6-foot stalks. By .3 mile you'll be back on the lakeshore where you turn right.

South across the 8-mile-long lake is a 60-acre island, covered with low grasses and shrubs on the north end and trees toward the south. If you have a canoe, the island invites another day's exploring. Power boats and water skiing are allowed in the wide channel southwest of the island, but only canoes or small boats with nearly-silent electric motors ply the waters near where you'll walk.

At .6 mile round a point northwest into a "no wake" boating area. Hundreds of tiny inlets and coves lure fishermen to the lake, which is stocked with walleye pike, pickerel, muskellunge, yellow perch, and other species. Although most fishermen use boats, many land-based anglers have beaten narrow paths along the shore.

Shoreline walking is easier than most bushwhacking because it avoids much of the underbrush. In summer, dry weather reduces the body of water somewhat, providing even more walking room. By 1 mile you've passed the worst of the underbrush. The lake here lines an old grassy field beginning to reforest, providing good cover for pheasants and rabbits. The old paved road leading down to the water's edge was abandoned when the lake was formed.

By 1.5 miles, the lake fingers narrow and the water depth quickly sinks to 45 feet with few shallows. Climb out on rocks over the water to watch yellow perch and crappies in deep pools along the edge. Muskellunge and walleyes are deep-water fish, but perch and crappies

travel in schools, preferring shallower water where they can easily hide from larger fish.

For hikers, wildlife around the lake is a major attraction. Tracks of raccoons, deer, fish-eating birds, and other shoreline feeders line the water's edge. In spring Blue Marsh Lake is a stopover for flocks of Canada geese, coots, bluebills, and other migratory waterfowl and land birds. I saw herring gulls, a wood duck, an osprey in the distance, and a belted kingfisher dive headfirst into the water for fish. A green heron—18 inches high with long legs and neck for capturing small frogs, fish, and crayfish—was startled into flight when it saw me. The great blue heron also stalks the shallower waters here.

At 2 miles PA 183 crosses an arm the lake. Turn left across the bridge, then left in winter or early spring before the forest floor rejuvenates. (Blue Marsh Lake makes an excellent cross-country or snowshoe trip, complete with frozen path to the large island.) Walk south along the water, turning right in .4 mile along the shoreline. You'll find heavy long pants welcome protection in this densely

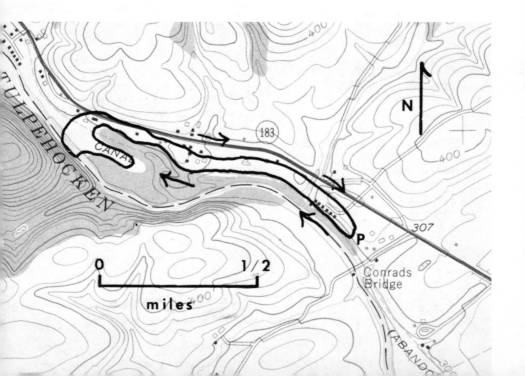

forested area where walking is slow, and herons and ospreys are likely sightings.

To return to PA 183 you can retrace your steps to the bridge, or leave the water's edge to head due north, reaching PA 183 in a shorter distance. Turn right at 2.6 miles and cross the bridge to a parking area on the right. Turn right on the old fern-lined road here. The road is now broken pavement with grass growing in the cracks but provides easier walking than bushwhacking.

At 3.5 miles leave the old road, turning left to continue south toward the lakeshore visible ahead. Turn left at the water to retrace your steps, but before you reach the first lake finger you rounded near the beginning of the hike, turn left again, leaving the lake for a shortcut back to your car. Cross the abandoned fields east to a small stand of white pines at 4.3 miles. At 4.9 miles you'll see the beach area and your car .1 mile ahead to the right.

USGS maps do not yet show newly constructed Blue Marsh Lake, but you can determine elevations and locations of abandoned roads from them. For a U.S. Army Corps of Engineers map and brochure write to Public Affairs Office, Army Engineers, Philadelphia District, Custom House, Second and Chestnut Streets, Philadelphia, PA 19106.

12

Philips Canyon

Total distance: 8.25 miles
Hiking time: 4 hours
Vertical rise: 600 feet
Maps: USGS 7½' Auburn; K.T.A. #3

Scrawled on a piece of notepad held down with a rock is this message: "7/2 Spring at Philips Canyon dry. Water no good at Neye's Shelter." You'll find this strenuous hike on the Appalachian Trail (AT) in the State Game Lands west of Allentown less like Death Valley than the note implies. You may have to bring your own water, but the area is surprisingly airy and cool, even on a hot, muggy summer day. A variety of mountainous terrain awaits you: dense scrub forest, game lands feed lots, and the deep, narrow Philips Canyon.

From east or west take exit 8 off US 22—I-78, north away from Shartlesville. In less than .5 mile go straight on another paved road at a sharp right bend, following signs north to the game lands boundary. Bear right at 1.2 miles. In .6 mile park at a gate barring vehicular traffic. From the north take PA 61 south from the Frackville exit on I-81, past the turnoff for Hawk Mountain (see Hike 14). When you reach US 22—I-78, 25 miles south of Pottsville, head west 6 miles to the Shartlesville exit and follow the rest of the driving instructions. From Reading take PA 61 north to US 22—I-78, continue west to exit 8, and follow directions to the trailhead.

Start north on the gravel road beyond the gate and climb Blue Mountain steadily. North Kill Creek, soon below you, rushes off to the left. At .2 mile the Sandy Spring Trail intersects and heads left downhill across the stream to join the AT 1.8 miles west. Before you reach the top of the mountain you'll pass several unmarked hunter's trails or very faded woods roads heading off both right and left. You won't find hunters in the game lands in summer, and hunting on Sunday is illegal in Pennsylvania.

Near North Kill Creek the hemlocks gradually give way to dense scrubby white pine and oak, birch, and mountain laurel—impossible to penetrate without a trail. Near the top of the mountain, the soil changes from peat to sand and vegetation shrinks to shrubs with a few tall pines.

The higher you climb, the better the view through a gap in the mountains on your left. Tall, gaunt tree skeletons in the hollow signal the area's wetness. A single strand of wire along the boundary to the left prohibits entry into a wildlife breeding area. At 1 mile turn right on another good gravel road, marked by a small green and white sign number 23. As I topped the rise three deer were calmly browsing at the edge of the road, secure in the open in this

remote area though it was nearly noon. Spotting me they stamped, snorted, and fled in a flurry of white tails.

Continue past feeding stations for turkeys and deer—simple wire barrels placed in pairs just off the road, stocked with hay and corn in winter by game commission officials. Further ahead, a cleared area on the right is sown with grain. From the top of one hill I counted five deer, far enough ahead to look more like grazing cattle than whitetails. The feed lots and barrels sustain more deer in the area than woods vegetation alone.

At 2 miles watch carefully for the AT intersection. Halfway up a hill on the left is a large post stuck into the ground, and immediately to the right a faint path crosses the narrow belt of grain. Turn right (south) into the woods at a 4-foot stone cairn blazed with the Appalachian Trail logo. The AT turns left (east) in .1 mile, parallel to the road. Softball-sized limestones in the path slow you down enough to enjoy a snack of ripe blueberries in late July from thick bushes beside the trail.

At 3 miles reach Philips Canyon. A sign on the right points 125 yards down a blue-blazed path to a seasonal spring. Leave your pack at the top of the canyon for the descent. The gorge is deep and narrow—even hemlocks and ferns can't soften the impression of large rocks and very steep grade. Water from the spring rushes down the wash. There is little resemblance between Philips Canyon and the Grand Canyon, or even Penn-

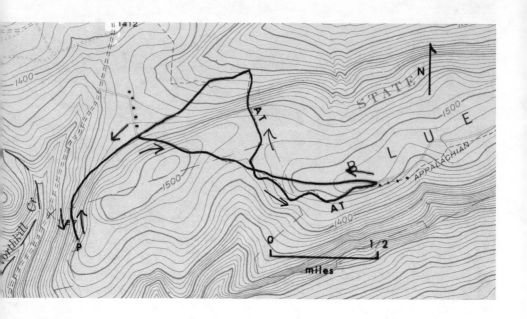

sylvania's Grand Canyon (Pine Creek Gorge in north central Pennsylvania). Philips Canyon—more like a very steep wash for runoff on Blue Mountain —surprises you because it's so different from what you expect in the mountains.

Climb out of the canyon carefully; loose rocks give way beneath your feet, and you should watch out for poisonous snakes. Return to the AT and continue east. Beyond the canyon, the trail begins to bear consistently left—east, northeast. Where the AT turns sharply right, a narrow, unmarked trail continues straight ahead. (Taking this path shortens your hike by 2 miles. The path seems to end in a grain field after 200 yards. Cross the narrow belt to the gravel road where the trees begin.)

To continue on the AT, turn sharply right. Dense forest blocks out long views. At 4 miles turn left (west) where the AT recrosses the wide gravel road. Pass the wide grain belt on the left, with clear vistas ahead along the top of the mountain. Deer and pheasants are likely sightings, and a

ruffed grouse—Pennsylvania's state bird—can be spotted taking a dust bath in the loose gravel on a warm day.

At 5.7 miles reach the AT crossing and stone cairn on the left. (Retracing your steps to the car from here will further shorten your hike.) For now turn right (north) on the AT. The flat ridge ends and the rocky woods trail drops 300 feet in .4 mile. At 6.1 miles the trail turns sharply left (west). The steep descent ends in .3 mile and you circle the mountain, turning right again at 6.4 miles downhill across Stony Creek, through mature oaks. At 6.8 miles pass Neye's Shelter and turn left.

Turn left (south) again at 7 miles, onto the gravel road you began hiking on. In .3 mile pass the intersection marked number 23, continuing .9 mile to your car at 8.25 miles. If you leave the AT just beyond Philips Canyon, your total mileage will be 6.25 miles. If you also continue on the gravel road instead of heading north on the AT on the return, your hike will total just under 6 miles.

13

Pulpit Rock and the Pinnacle

Total distance: 8.9 miles
Hiking time: 5½ hours
Vertical rise: 1,000 feet
Maps: USGS 7½' Hamburg; K.T.A. #2

Wait for the clearest day of the year to hike this strenuous circuit on the Appalachian Trail (AT) 25 miles west of Allentown. You'll need strong lungs and tough feet because this demanding hike gains 1,000 feet in 2 miles—climbing and teetering over obstructing rocks that threaten to twist an ankle. Your double reward is one of the most panoramic views in eastern Pennsylvania, 200 degrees of visibility from the two rock outcrops on Blue Mountain, looking east to Allentown and north to the Poconos.

To reach the trailhead from the west, take the Hamburg exit off US 22—I-78 south into town, turning left (east) at the first stoplight, on to the old Baltimore Road toward Lenhartsville. In 3 miles turn left again just beyond Saint Paul's Church. Cross underneath US 22—I-78 in .5 mile, continuing to Hamburg Reservoir where the road ends at a gate. Daytime parking only is allowed here. From Allentown drive west on US 22—I-78 to exit 11, continue .5 mile south into Lenhartsville, and turn west on Baltimore Road. In 3 miles reach Saint Paul's Church where you turn right. From Reading drive 20 miles to Hamburg on PA 61, turn right on Baltimore Road, and left at the church in 3 miles.

Walk around the gate barring the dirt road to begin your hike. In .25 mile the Appalachian Trail cuts across your path at Windsor Furnace, the remains of a nineteenth-century iron-smelting furnace. The AT to the right will be your return trail from the Pinnacle and Pulpit Rock. For now, continue .1 mile to an intersection at the reservoir. The right fork follows the west side of the fenced basin, but your route heads left (northwest) uphill. Once the main AT route, this side trail with faded, far-spaced blue blazes climbs steadily through thick oak and birch woods. Thanks to patient, long-ago road builders, the footing is good on this woods road lined with football-sized limestones thrown here and there on the upside of the roadbed.

On top of the ridge at 2 miles the dense forest gives way to scrub growth. Turn right (east) here along the white-blazed AT, a wide, grassy woods road. Frogs and spring peepers gather near skunk cabbage in a few low areas soggy from small springs. Drier sections of the road are lined with blueberry bushes or stunted laurel where the sun can penetrate the thick forest.

After 2 easy, flat miles along the top of Blue Mountain, the road ends at 4 miles. The AT continues ahead on a path where rocks stick up like needles in a pincushion and slow your pace. As the path gets more rock strewn, look up from your feet occasionally to notice how the mountain ridge is narrowing. On either side of the trail are sheer drop-offs, though except perhaps in winter, the dense forest does not permit vistas.

At 4.8 miles you'll reach the Pinnacle, 250 feet left of the main trail on a blue-blazed path. Climb right out to the edge of the outcropping beyond the trees for the breathtaking view. To the left is Hawk Mountain (see Hike 14) with its own vast rock outcroppings on the peak. The typical mountain shape in this part of Pennsylvania is a long and narrow razorback ridge. Each sharp fold runs southwest-northeast, from the south central border to the northeast corner of the state. Sedimentary rocks were forced upward by a cataclysmic uplift, forming the mountains. Erosion has cut valleys

into the soft rock beds but left the hard strata as a wide band of uniformly folded ridges.

Freightcar-sized blocks on the Pinnacle's edge look as though they're balanced precariously on each other. The outcropping extends about 50 feet beyond the trees before dropping in a sheer fall to the valley below. Watch where you put your feet and hands and where you sit on boulders; both copperheads and rattlesnakes can be found here. Smaller ridges beyond the trees are cleared and cultivated, one planted in a circular pattern like a giant fingerprint to prevent erosion. The outcropping to the right (southwest), 2.1 miles away via the AT, is Pulpit Rock.

Return to the junction with the AT to follow the rocky rim of Blue Mountain to Pulpit Rock on what was once an AT side trail called the Valley Rim Trail. This toughest section of the hike starts out

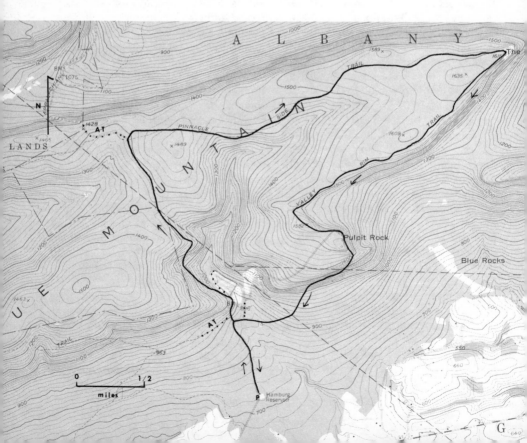

easily enough—slightly downhill on a narrow path white with laurel blooms in May. The footing gets progressively worse as you near the Pulpit. Rocks of all sizes pepper the path so thickly that a step on bare ground is a novelty.

As you near Pulpit Rock you'll pass several unnamed outcroppings with good vistas but not the scope of the Pinnacle. At 6.6 miles the trail turns sharply left, still along the rim. From here to Pulpit Rock elevation change is minimal but rocks are a constant obstacle. Pass several more rock outcrops with limited views, reaching Pulpit Rock at 7 miles. While I rested for lunch one hot Tuesday, ten rock climbers groped their way up the sheer face of the Pulpit. But the view back to the Pinnacle drew my attention away from the climbers. What looks like a grass-covered ski slope between the two outcroppings is actually a band of rocks 200 to 600 feet wide and nearly .5 mile long known as the Blue Rocks. They were formed when quartzite boulders 4 inches to 20 feet in diameter moved down over unanchored shale from the mountains above, covering the area to a depth of 30 feet. Boulder Field (see

Hike 39) and the River of Rocks on Hawk Mountain were similarly formed. According to geologists, running water can be heard beneath the rocks, which were already in place before the mature oak forest now covering the slopes appeared.

From Pulpit Rock back to your car is another 2 miles. Just beyond the overlook the AT turns right downhill, away from the rim. Down the trail 100 yards is an old astronomical observatory—two short aluminum buildings that resemble silos. Behind the observatory a narrow road leads back to the parking area.

Continue down the mountain on the AT. Just below the observatory you'll reach an intersection with the still passable old AT on the right—.8 mile shorter and a sharper descent than the relocation made in 1978. Stay on the new, blazed section, which soon becomes a pleasant two-track. At 8.6 miles turn left on a wider dirt road; to the right 500 feet is an overnight shelter for hikers. Continue on the AT .2 mile to Windsor Furnace, turn left, and retrace the last .5 mile to your car.

14

Hawk Mountain Sanctuary

Total distance: 1.5 miles
Hiking time: all day
Vertical rise: 300 feet
Maps: USGS 7½' New Ringgold; sanctuary map

During the spring and fall migrations, thousands of hawk fanciers from all over the world visit Hawk Mountain Sanctuary, a 2,000-acre privately maintained wildlife refuge 20 miles west of Allentown and 50 miles east of Harrisburg. Atop the North Lookout the ridges to the east lead out for 70 miles on a clear day. The day goes quickly, punctuated by cries of "Bird over number 2" followed by an orchestrated turning of binoculars. A lucky watcher will see thousands of hawks, and perhaps an eagle. Few hawks were in the air the day I came, but one was the endangered peregrine falcon, almost unknown in the East today.

In the 1920s and 30s, hawk-shooting on Hawk Mountain was a major local business; ammunition companies hauled wagons to the mountains and sold shot to hunters who came by the hundreds. In 1934, when the sanctuary was established, caretaker Maurice Broun faced threats from irate hunters.

Today, the hawks have only to keep an eye out for overzealous birders perched in trees on the pinnacles. You find hundreds of people here on a September week-end—weekdays are quieter. The spring migration brings fewer hawks and fewer hawk fanciers. May also brings migrating warblers and showy displays of rhododendron, mountain laurel, and flowering dogwood. A low-pressure weather system heading south across the mountains produces good flights of hawks several days after it passes. In September and October, winds from the northwest are favorable, and warm days with southerly winds bring the hawks north again in spring. Rain or no wind will ground the birds. September brings ospreys, broad-winged and sharp-shinned hawks, and rarely, a bald eagle. The greatest variety of hawks pass in October, and red-tailed hawks and golden eagles in November.

From Allentown, drive west 30 miles on US 22—I-78 to PA 61. Turn north and continue 4 miles to PA 895. Turn right (northeast), reaching Drehersville in 2 miles, where the sanctuary is a well-marked right turn. Continue 1 mile up a steep, winding road that tops Hawk Mountain. Turn right down the well-marked entrance road and park in the lot.

From Reading, drive PA 61 north 24 miles to PA 895 where you turn right and follow the rest of the driving instructions. From Philadelphia, take US 422 to Reading where you join PA 61 north. From Scranton, take I-81 south to Frackville,

turn south on PA 61, and continue 20 miles. Just past Molino turn left (northeast) on PA 895. From Harrisburg, take I-81 north to US 22—I-78; continue on US 22—I-78 to PA 61, turn north, and follow the directions to the parking lot.

The trailhead and the museum headquarters are at the far side of the parking lot, east of the sanctuary entrance. Admission is free to the small museum, open daily from 8 A.M. to 5 P.M. Find the orange-blazed trail on the parking lot side of the headquarters and begin walking north. In 100 yards, cross the road to a small wooden pavillion where you pay the entrance fee and receive a map.

Although signs warn those improperly dressed to turn back, the .7 mile up to the North Lookout is easy footing: a broad path of wood chips or sand. Bring a day pack equipped for a day on a windy, exposed outcrop: binoculars, field guide to birds, water, lunch, windbreaker, sunglasses, and brimmed hat. At .2 mile reach the South Lookout. To the east you look down into a wide hollow and the River of Rocks, a glaciated relic with the same geologic history as Boulder Field in Hickory Run State Park (see Hike 39), which winds like a narrow river down to the agricultural valley below. To the north is Hawk Mountain (part of the Kittatinny Ridge), rising several hundred feet above you.

At .6 mile the trail splits to rejoin on the North Lookout. The shorter trail to the right rises more steeply; instead, take the longer, easier trail to the left. The dense labyrinthine formations of white Tuscarora sandstone, called Hall of the Mountain King, are the remains of sand mining operations in the nineteenth century.

Just beyond the labyrinth, wood and stone steps take you to the crest of the mountain and the North Lookout. Walk to your right toward a huge outcropping where boulders form convenient seats for birders. The view is wide angle, over 200 degrees of visibility north to the Poconos and east to Allentown. To your right (southeast) are Hemlock Heights, Owls Head beyond, and the most distant, the Pinnacle (see Hike 13).

It may take you a moment to understand what goes on atop Hawk Mountain on a fall weekend. Cries of "Sharpie over number 2" produce pairs of binoculars trained on the spot. In the parlance of the sanctuary, the mountain ridges to the east are numbered: the one furthest away is number 1, followed by numbers 2, 3, 4, and 5. If someone reports a bird over number 1, you know immediately where to look. You have to be sharp eyed to spot the nearly invisible black speck before anyone else, or to identify the speck as a *sharpie* (sharp-shinned hawk).

Dedicated birders say the most exciting sighting is a *plank*—an eagle with wings straight across. The inverted gull-wing shape of the turkey vulture is also easy to spot. To clear the ridges, the hawks *kettle*—find a thermal or warm patch of air, and circle tightly upward twenty to

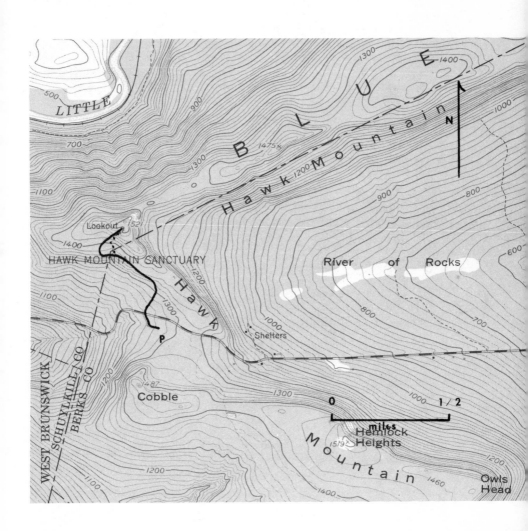

thirty times before soaring off over the mountain. Several times I saw a sharpie painstakingly gain altitude only to fold its wings and dive like a bullet into another hawk.

Shortly after I arrived someone called out, "Bird over number 1." Someone further down the outcropping claimed it a falcon. A few seconds later, "It's a really *big* falcon!" The bird was flapping southward, just above the Pinnacle. Falcons are fast-flying birds. Unlike many hawks, they rarely soar, and flapping is a key to early identification. A "big falcon" meant a peregrine falcon, an extremely rare bird. Peregrine sightings, even at Hawk Mountain, are not common, and the sight of this handsome bird flapping calmly southward was a rare experience.

In late afternoon, return down the mountain via the same route. No pets are allowed and people have a tendency to whisper here. Children willing to be quiet for several hours could hike to the North Lookout, and even nonhikers should be able to negotiate the easy walk to South Lookout. The beauty of Hawk Mountain lies not in a difficult climb but in the extraordinary vistas that captivate you even on a good hawking day. But the hawks themselves are the real attraction of the sanctuary. Watching them calmly and regally work their way through the thermals above the valley is a thrill no outdoor lover should miss.

Susquehanna
East

15

Middle Creek Wildlife Management Area

Total distance: 3.9 miles
Hiking time: 1¾ hours
Vertical rise: 250 feet
Maps: USGS 7½' Richland, USGS 7½' Womelsdorf

From the moment you step out of your car, the sounds of the 4,000 Canada geese that breed at Middle Creek Wildlife Management Area will be with you. The preserve, between Lebanon and Reading on the Lebanon-Lancaster county line, is a tract of more than 5,000 acres of fields and ponds administered by the Pennsylvania Game Commission for the protection, propagation, and harvest of wildlife. In season, tens of thousands of geese cover the lake—made by the impoundment of Middle Creek—and the surrounding fields. Mallards, teal, snow geese, buffle-heads—nearly every kind of waterfowl found in Pennsylvania— pause here during their spring and fall migrations along the Atlantic flyway north to breeding grounds in Canada, or south to wintering areas in Florida.

In fall, the north side of the lake fills with hunters awarded one-day goose permits in a state-wide lottery. In the southern section where this hike begins, hunting is also permitted. Fall is not the best time to hike here, unless you go on Sunday when hunting is illegal in Pennsylvania.

Middle Creek is most easily reached from Kleinfeltersville, 1 mile north of the area's entrance, and 3.1 miles from the trailhead. From Lebanon (on US 322)

take PA 897 southeast 10 miles to Kleinfeltersville. If you are driving from Reading, take PA 422 west 8 miles to Wernersville. Head south on an un-numbered road, avoiding left-hand turnoffs for Fritztown and Reinholds at 3 and 5 miles. At 7 miles join PA 897 and drive northwest 8 miles to Klein-feltersville. North of Lancaster, PA 501 joins PA 897 in 14 miles. Continue 2 miles east on PA 897 to Kleinfeltersville.

Kleinfeltersville's only south-turning street is the access road into the management area; watch for the large sign to Middle Creek at the intersection. Drive 2.2 miles to the visitor's center on the right, open from March 1 to November 30. Continue .9 mile beyond the visitor's center to the Greenbriar Picnic Area road, near the dam. Turn right and continue 100 yards to the parking lot.

This loop hike connecting four Middle Creek trails begins on the Valley View Trail, which takes off from treeline on the western perimeter of the picnic area's graded lawn. The trailhead is not marked, but the well-worn path is blazed with yellow metal triangles tacked to trees. Head south on the rocky and occasionally steep trail, to the top of the ridge visible from the picnic area. Crest Black Oak

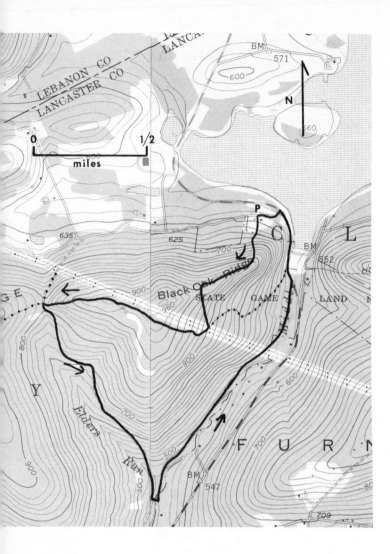

Ridge at .2 mile and bear right around large boulders, past mature hickory and oak trees.

On the crest, a log bench invites views of the entire lake and surrounding fields. Even here, .5 mile from the lakeshore, the calls of Canada geese and noisy mallards reach your ears. The trail follows the ridge for another .4 mile, leaving it near a small stand of hemlocks to head left downhill.

The Valley View Trail ends at .8 mile, intersecting the Horseshoe Trail, a 121 mile trail extending west from Valley Forge (see Hike 5) to its endpoint on the Appalachian Trail near the Susquehanna River just north of Harrisburg (see Hike 50). The Horseshoe Trail, designed for trail riding, is also well traveled by hikers. At this intersection, you can shorten your hike to 1.5 miles if you turn left, follow the trail back out to the access road, and continue .3 mile back to your car. Instead, turn right to begin a gentle climb. Bear left and cross a wide power-line cut before reentering the woods.

In this section of the wildlife management area, several feed lots—small cleared areas sown with buckwheat —attract and maintain wildlife in a population density higher than that found in natural woods. Within several yards I saw grouse, deer, squirrels, and woodpeckers; you are also likely to see or hear woodcocks, turkeys, and rabbits.

Across the power-line cut, the Horse-shoe Trail widens into a smooth, grassy path—a relief from the rocky and sometimes slippery Valley View Trail. You soon top another ridge, and at 1.3 miles reach a trail intersection. About 100 yards to the left another feed lot winds around the hillside. Deer frequently gather at the end of the field, where a quiet walk is likely to produce a view of flagging tails. To the right a few steps, another excellent view of the lake area extends north all the way to Kleinfeltersville.

Continue straight ahead, and slowly descend a stretch of rockier trail. After a steeper section, reach a trail crossing at 1.7 miles. Here turn sharply left downhill on the unmarked Elder Run Trail, avoiding

another feed lot. Shortly you'll pass an overnight shelter; just beyond on the right are a springhouse and the remains of a brick chimney. Below the shelter the rocky trail parallels Elder Run, a narrow stream rushing through ferns and moss. The .9 mile Elder Run Trail ends just beyond a bridge over Elder Run.

Turn left on the clearly-marked Middle Creek Trail, which follows a nineteenth-century trolly line, straight and flat though sometimes rocky. In places, the rotted ties of the trolly are visible through the rocky undergrowth. Past a 50-foot soggy section, overgrown with briars, the trail ends on the access road. Turn left, pass the dam impoundment, and reach the road into the picnic area in .3 mile. Turn left and find your car in 100 yards.

In a recent National Geographic Society book, *Back Roads America*, Thomas O'Neill describes his journey through rural eastern Pennsylvania, attracted to Middle Creek Wildlife Management Area by honking Canada geese overhead. He writes that nearby Amish residents are also drawn to Middle Creek: "The wildlife area's nearness and noncommercial nature make it popular among Lancaster County's Amish and Mennonite families, who sometimes come here to ramble, picnic, or play softball or volleyball."

3/16 Sweet hike poorly marked

16

Kettle Run

Total distance: 4 miles
Hiking time: 2 hours
Vertical rise: 550 feet
Maps: USGS 7½' Manheim, USGS 7½' Lititz

A spectacular view of lush Lancaster Valley farmlands highlights this hike in the Furnace Hills section of State Game Lands 156. The circuit hike between Lebanon and Lancaster includes a steady climb to the top of a forested ridge, a visit to a lookout tower, and a sharp descent over sometimes slippery rocks.

To reach the game lands from Harrisburg or Philadelphia, take the Pennsylvania Turnpike (I-76) to exit 20, where you join PA 72 north. In 2 miles turn right (east) onto US 322 and drive 4 miles. Just before US 322 crosses Walnut Run at the Lebanon Pumping Station, turn right on Township Route 560, which follows the creek a short distance. In 1 mile you'll reach the game lands parking lot on the right.

This hike leaves the north side of the parking lot on a wide gravel road now blocked to motor vehicles by a gate. Begin a steady pull uphill, northwest, crossing the bridge over Kettle Run at .4 mile. You'll pass several open areas, feed lots for deer in the game lands. At .8 mile reach a sign pointing to a path leaving the road uphill. Turn right on the narrow path that smooths and widens once you are through the underbrush along the road. For the first 1 mile the oak and maple

forest is broken by several small, open glades dotted with wide hummocks of moss and grass, bright green even in winter.

In the light snow cover I saw tracks of rabbit, deer, fox, and pheasant crisscrossing the entire area. Continue uphill, past the edge of an old field where most of the deer tracks led. The trail bends left to enter a mature oak and hickory forest, reaching the top of a small hill and then descending. Here I saw rabbit tracks again; beside and on top of them were fox tracks. Further on I spotted a rabbit bouncing easily ahead of me on the path.

The inclines and descents here are slight, but the countryside is rolling enough to make an interesting cross-country skiing trip in winter. Near the bottom of the incline the trail becomes slightly boggy where a small spring has soaked the ground. Winter-killed ferns here indicate the area is alive with fiddleheads—as well as spring peepers—by April or May.

At 1.1 miles avoid a dead end off to the right through a section of trees that even in winter look dead. It's possible this circular hollow is wet enough in spring to kill the oaks and pines here. Bear left and begin a steady climb, winding around the hollow

until you reach a paved road and the Horseshoe Trail at 1.8 miles.

Turn left and follow the yellow-blazed Horseshoe Trail west along the forest-lined, narrow road to Cornwall Lookout Tower at 2.6 miles. The tower is old, rickety, and wooden—but if you can stand the creaking, the view at the top is impressive. To the south the fertile Lancaster Valley with its miles of farmlands and fields spreads out before you. Elevation at the tower is just under 1,200 feet, 700 feet above the valley below.

Continue on the road past the tower .25 mile to a power station and power-line cut. Here, a faint, unmarked trail leads left down the cut on a steep and rocky hill. If you couldn't quite bring yourself to climb the old lookout tower you'll get another chance at a splendid view of the valley, when the hill ends and starts downward. The rocks are very slippery when wet; here heavy-soled boots make the going easier and safer. The drop to the road below is steep but the worst is over in .4 mile. Continue across a field of boulders for another .1 mile to reach a gravel road, the same one you began your hike on. Turn

left to finish your 1.7 mile walk back to the car.

Dense woods crowd the road on both sides, and deer hurry out of your path just ahead. The road is a gradual downhill grade, with spots where you can see for quite a distance ahead—ideal for sighting deer. Pennsylvania's game lands should be avoided for hiking at least on the opening days of small game and deer season. Hunting is prohibited on Sundays, however, and Kettle Run is a perfect Sunday afternoon outing.

At 3.2 miles the thick woods end and are replaced by scrubby growth, tall grass, boulders, and underbrush. Even in winter, this area is alive with small birds: tufted titmice, white-throated sparrows, slate-colored juncos, and others. I walked in and sat on a boulder, scattering the birds. In a few minutes they were back, feeding and scratching as before, not noticing me at all. The titmice were the shyest, but juncos and black-capped chickadees often came within 8 to 10 feet of where I was sitting.

Reach Kettle Run at 3.6 miles and the gate at 4 miles. Your car will be straight ahead.

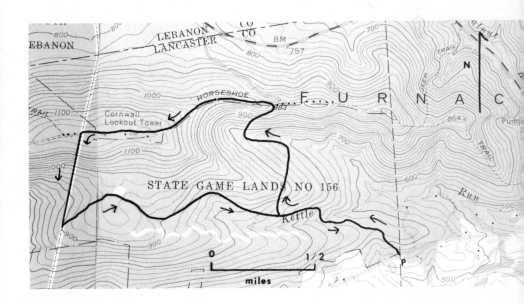

17

Kellys Run Natural Area

Total distance: 5 miles
Hiking time: 2½ hours
Vertical rise: 500 feet
Maps: USGS 7½' Holtwood; Conestoga Trail map

Part of the National Recreational Trail System, the Kellys Run-Pinnacle Trail offers challenging hiking and birding as well as stunning views of the Susquehanna River at Pinnacle Overlook. The trail crosses land owned mainly by the Pennsylvania Power and Light Company (PP&L), which has a power-generating plant further south on the river. Kellys Run is part of the Conestoga Trail (see Hike 48), a rugged 15-mile trail built by the Lancaster Hiking Club on PP&L land, from Martic Forge in Lancaster County south to Lock 12 across the Susquehanna in York County. For a map of the entire Conestoga Trail (including Kellys Run), write George Aukamp, Lake Aldred Supt., PA Power and Light Co., Holtwood, PA 17352, or telephone.

To reach the trailhead take PA 74 southeast 23 miles from York to PA 372, turn left, and cross the Susquehanna River on the Norman Wood Bridge. Turn left on Crystal Drive in 2 miles, the second left beyond the river. Drive 1.5 miles to where the road ends at the Holtwood Recreation Area parking lot, near Holtwood Arboretum. From Lancaster take PA 272 south 13 miles to Buck, turn right on PA 372, and continue 6 miles to Crystal Drive (intersection marked). Turn right to reach

the parking lot at the recreation area. Water is available both here and at Pinnacle Overlook.

This hike begins on a worn path at the picnic pavilion to the right (east), beyond a large wooden sign showing trails in the area. At the edge of the lawn enter an overgrown field where tall grass harbors ticks in late spring and early summer. You'll cover most of the distance to Pinnacle Overlook on the orange-blazed Conestoga Trail, but don't rely entirely on the blazes. Trees may also carry blazes of other colors, marking a variety of trails. In several hundred yards the trail descends to stands of small white pine, then mature oak.

Enroute to Kellys Run, make your way down a steep hillside covered with huge, gnarled laurel. In late May and June when the laurel blooms and the stream runs deep and full, hiking is spectacular here. Deciduous tree leaves aren't fully developed yet, opening views of the Susquehanna. Summer is somewhat less pleasant—snakes are more plentiful and the area can be extremely hot—but fall and winter are excellent hiking seasons.

Reach Kellys Run at .75 mile and turn left downstream into Holtwood Gorge through hemlocks and boulders. At 1 mile the creek bends sharply left ninety degrees, just past a sheer 40-foot rock outcropping nearly hidden by dense hemlock and laurel. Cross the stream (no bridge); this can be difficult in high water. Once safely across, turn left and continue downstream as the trail narrows and the stream widens, coursing through this scenic glen in its rush to empty into the Susquehanna.

At 1.5 miles the trail splits. The Conestoga Trail continues downhill along the creek and your trail leads sharply uphill to the right away from the rocky and frequently slippery creek. In .1 mile several paths intersect on top of a knoll. Turn sharply right (north) uphill again. In 150 yards reach a marked intersection; turn left on the Pinnacle Trail. The Pine Tree Trail to the right takes .5 mile longer to reach Pinnacle Overlook, and doesn't have the grand views of the Susquehanna.

The nearly flat old woods road winds around the mountain, in .2 mile crossing a narrow woods road and ascending a series of shallow wooden steps. About 100 yards past the road, reach another intersection where you'll turn right; the loop to the left eventually returns to the

Pinnacle Trail further on. This area atop the bluff was once a farm or orchard—at one point a long stone fence obligingly breaks at the path and continues on the other side. This wild, overgrown land—alive with warblers in the tangle of vines—is hard to imagine under cultivation. To the west the land falls away to the Susquehanna.

Reach the Pinnacle Overlook at 2.2 miles where the trail ends in a parking area amid picnic tables. You are 500 feet above Lake Aldred Gorge, a backup of the Susquehanna River. Because of Holtwood Dam 2 miles south, the water depth in this narrow .25-mile-wide bend drops to 190 feet from the Susquehanna's usual shallow 6 feet. To the north, Reed Island sits in the middle of the river and Hartman Island hugs the shoreline. These and several unnamed island rock outcrops are gathering spots for waterfowl: herring gulls, trumpeter swans, Canada geese, great blue herons, green herons, American egrets, and many others. In summer you may see hawks or an osprey soaring here before their fall migration south.

For your return, wind south along the

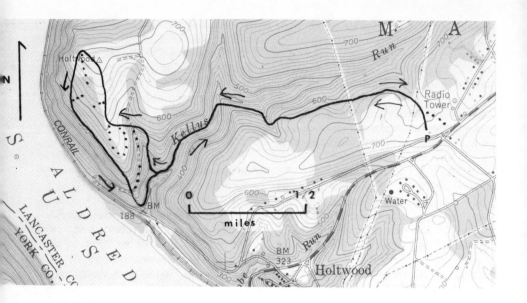

river side of the hill on the Fire Line Trail. The trail begins where the Pinnacle Trail ends (on the right as you face south), and is marked by another large wooden trail sign. The broad path along the very edge of the ridge provides nearly continuous views of the river, especially south toward the dam and power plant, and across the river to the opposite tree-covered hills and cliffs. Pass one trail intersection and soon rejoin the Conestoga Trail to the right, turning sharply downhill along a power-line cut overlooking the power plant.

Follow the Conestoga Trail for .3 mile, nearly to the river's edge at 3.1 miles. Here, make a sharp left to follow Kellys Run back upstream. After .2 mile along the rocky, noisy run you'll reach the intersection where you left the Conestoga Trail to climb to Pinnacle Overlook. Retrace your steps the last 1.7 miles—up Kellys Run and the laurel hillside, through the pines, and across the field. In season, check for ticks when you reach your car.

18

Susquehannock State Park

Total distance: 2.5 miles
Hiking time: 1¼ hours
Vertical rise: 400 feet
Maps: USGS 7½' Holtwood; state park map

Sweeping views of the mile-wide Susquehanna River and impressive stands of rhododendron make this short circuit hike in Susquehannock State Park south of Lancaster a memorable walk. You'll find it easy to spend a whole day hiking here, winding along a fast-rushing stream through hills of holly, skirting the edge of an old field.

To reach this small, 224-acre park in southern Lancaster County near the Mason-Dixon Line, take PA 74 southeast 3 miles from York, heading east into Lancaster County on PA 372 via the Norman Wood Bridge. Across the river continue 4 miles, turning right onto Susquehannock Drive. Drive 3 miles to the park sign and turn right. From Lancaster, take PA 272 south 18 miles (4 miles beyond Buck) to Silver Springs Road. Turn right and drive 1 mile, turning left on Susquehannock Drive. Continue 2 miles to the park entrance, turn right, and drive 1.5 miles to reach the parking lots.

The Scenic View Trail leaves the west end of the parking lot, marked by a large trail sign. Walk 150 yards to the edge of the bluffs for a fine view of the Susquehanna several hundred feet below, then right 150 yards to another overlook. Several small, unnamed, rocky

islands on the river provide safety for egrets, swans, geese—and herring gulls that fly up from the Chesapeake Bay daily to feed.

Leave the river view to retrace your path 20 yards to the Fire Trail, marked by a post on your left. Hikers have worn many unofficial paths in the park, which often require slipping and scrambling over rocks and fallen trees. In contrast, park-made trails are wide, usually blazed, and easier to follow. Stay on the blazed Fire Trail, an old woods two-track with grass between the ruts, for .2 mile through quiet woods.

Reach the Plate's Eddy Trail, a sharp left-hand turn downhill on an unmarked but still recognizable path. If you're hiking with young children, you may want to avoid this steep and rocky turnoff. Named for the nineteenth-century Plate's Eddy Inn at the confluence of Wissler Run and the Susquehanna, which catered in the 1870s to raftsmen floating logs down the river, the Plate's Eddy Trail winds north downhill .3 mile to Wissler Run.

At the creek's edge turn right on the white-blazed Five Points Trail, which follows roughly the northern perimeter of the park. Hikers' trails here may cause some difficulty. Even the occasional white blazes don't completely prevent confusion about the right path through the boulders, downed hemlocks, and crisscrossing trails. Even more serious, the very steep slope down to the creek is ripe for erosion of the fragile topsoil. The boulders help prevent soil loss, but hikers can be even more helpful by sticking to the main trail. If you lose the trail, just keep following the creek upstream. Use caution on steep trail angles, wet and slippery here long after a rain. You'll find this section the roughest of the hike.

Between .5 mile and .6 mile you'll pass several trails to the right; at .6 mile the Pine Tree and Rhododendron trails head off right as one trail but soon split. All along the way, massive rhododendron competes with boulders and hemlocks for space on the rocky hill above you. At this intersection, rhododendron has completely taken over and blankets the hill. If you're hiking during late May and June, turn onto the Rhododendron Trail for an alternate .5 mile path through the very heart of these flowering evergreen shrubs. Near the top of the hill are stands of holly, less numerous than the rhododendron.

For this hike, however, continue ahead on the white-blazed Five Points Trail. In .1 mile the hill ends along a flat, wide creek bed. Wildflowers bloom profusely in the swampy bottom from the end of April into May: spring-beauties, saw-toothed violets, wood-sorrel, and Jack-in-the-pulpits. At .8 mile the trail crosses the tributary of Wissler Run. There's no bridge so you're on your own, but the crossing shouldn't be difficult unless the water is high after a rain. Across the stream, climb uphill into a more mature forest where deer tracks are abundant, and underbrush and boulders less so.

In .25 mile, reach the area of Five Points Property Corner, where property lines of five different owners once intersected—just before the trail makes a hairpin curve to the right, then turns sharply left in .1 mile. By 1.25 miles the trail heads downhill again—southeast, then southwest to recross the stream at 1.5 miles. Just beyond, the Five Points Trail ends on the Rhododendron Trail. Turn south here, avoiding the Spring Trail on the left. The Rhododendron Trail ends at 1.7 miles, between the park office on the

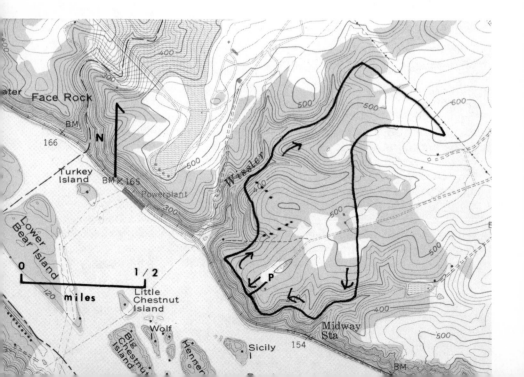

right and the old stone Landis House.

Complete the southern loop of your hike by crossing the paved entrance road to enter a baseball field and play area. At the edge of the woods on your left, pick up the Landis Trail, which runs .3 mile south to a spring and old chimney. The hemlocks, pines, and large white oaks of the northern half of the park give way here to small oaks, maples, and beeches.

The Landis Trail turns right at 2 miles, onto a section of trail open for horseback riding as well as hiking. (At 2.2 miles, a yellow-blazed trail to the right offers a shortcut. Turn left when the path ends in .1 mile, then almost immediately right onto the Overlook Trail. If you fail to turn right, you'll circle back on the Landis Trail.) For now, stay on the Landis Trail and swing north to join the Overlook Trail, a left turn.

The overlook is another .25 mile ahead at 2.4 miles. The round island to the left is Mount Johnson Island, the world's first bald eagle sanctuary. No eagles have been spotted here for years, but waterfowl, including whistling and mute swans—American egrets in summer, can be seen almost year-round. In April, I saw snow geese heading north. They can be distinguished in flight from Canada geese by their lighter color and unusual honking.

From the overlook, turn around and walk 150 yards through the picnic tables back to the parking lot.

84 *Susquehanna East*

19

Otter Creek

Total distance: 4 miles
Hiking time: 2 hours
Vertical rise: 120 feet
Maps: USGS 7½' Safe Harbor, USGS 7½' Airville

This hike in southern York County along the west bank of the Susquehanna River combines three short loops. You'll hike to Urey Lookout where the view differs little from frontier days, walk along fast-running, hemlock-shrouded Otter Creek, and trek through oaken woods to a pretty waterfall and pool. Logging has recently affected parts of this trail system on State Game Lands 83 and Pennsylvania Power and Light Company (PP&L) land, so you may find conditions somewhat different from these trail directions. Hiking during hunting season is not advised, except on Sundays when hunting is prohibited.

To reach Otter Creek, drive PA 74 southeast 11 miles from York. Just past Keys, turn left on the New Bridgeville road. Turn right on PA 425 in New Bridgeville and continue southeast 7 miles to the well-marked Otter Creek Recreation Area, built by PP&L. PA 425 leads downhill to the Susquehanna to cross Otter Creek, its small tributary. Park in the lot just across the bridge. The Otter Creek campground 150 yards beyond would also be a good base for hiking at nearby Kellys Run Natural Area and Susquehannock State Park (see Hikes 17 and 18). From Lancaster, take PA 272

south 14 miles to PA 372, turn right, and drive 7 miles to PA 74. Turn right again, following PA 74 north 5 miles to PA 425, turn right, and reach Otter Creek in 3 miles.

For now, avoid the trail along Otter Creek left of the parking lot. Walk back out to PA 425, turn left, and cross the bridge—then turn right, toward the river, and walk along the bank a few steps to an unpaved road at .1 mile. The Urey Islands are just offshore. Turn left on the unpaved road, winding uphill, slightly away from the river. When the road angles left at .25 mile, watch on the right for a narrow trail .3 mile uphill to the lookout—pleasant walking through pines and large oaks. Rocks spread on either side as you gain nearly 100 feet of altitude.

The view from Urey Lookout is impressive: northwest is Weise Island, to the south the five Urey Islands hug the shoreline like barrier reefs. At floodtime the shallow Susquehanna inundates the greenery-covered islands, preventing large tree growth. The small, rockier islands attract crowds of herring gulls, geese, mallards, and in summer, American egrets.

Return to Otter Creek on a less dramatic trail west and parallel to the one you

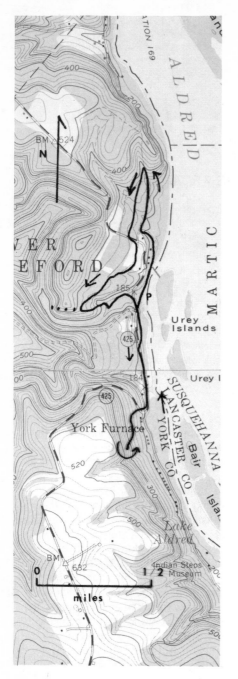

climbed. Retrace your path 100 yards to the split; bear right downhill through cool pines to reach the unpaved road at .8 mile. You have two choices here: turn left to retrace your steps to the parking lot, or right to reach PA 425 in 100 yards. Otter Creek is .2 mile to the left.

Back in the parking lot at 1 mile, walk west to the rugged but beautiful trail up Otter Creek. Hemlocks bow close to the water here, and cascading falls rush noisily along the creek. The high hill on the left reaches nearly straight up; to the right the boulder-filled, twisting creek narrows in places, widens and calms in others. Beside the trail, ferns and violets surround limestone boulders. Rocks and fallen trees can make this short stretch seem strenuous, even with little elevation change.

At 1.3 miles reach a trail intersection. Although you can continue upstream, walking becomes increasingly difficult as the hillsides plummet to the water, with no flat walking rim. Turn left, away from the creek, and switchback uphill to a dirt road at 1.5 miles. Logging and construction prevented me from completing the .75-mile stretch on the pine ridge above Otter Creek and the loop back to Otter Creek via Sawmill Run. If the two-track is still disturbed by logging, turn left on the dirt road and return .25 mile to the Susquehanna River near your car, at 1.75 miles. (If no logging is apparent at the intersection, turn right to continue to the end of the two-track, turn left, and in .25 mile cross Sawmill Run on the bridge. Turn left again beyond the run and walk 1.2 miles east to PA 425 and the Susquehanna. Return north on PA 425 to your car.)

Back on PA 425 near your car, head east down to the riverbank, then south, where only a 50-foot channel separates you from one of the large Urey Islands. Along the river channel I intruded on an anxious whistling swan—apparently with a mate nesting nearby. Whistling swans are smaller and do not have the graceful S-curved neck of the mute swans familiar in parks, with black bills instead of orange. This male scolded me with wings outspread in aggressive display until I was well past his territory.

After .5 mile along the river, reach the Indian Steps Museum. Once the summer home of a York lawyer at the turn of the century, this is now a private museum of his Indian artifacts collection. Across from the museum a trail leads west uphill into beautiful oak woods above the river. The well-maintained trail ascends through ferns and violets to a tiny run at 2.5 miles. Here, a 15-foot rock shelf drops a pretty trickle into a large, clear pool of spring water. Though a sign declares this Indian Maiden Falls, that waterfall is actually 1.2 miles south of the museum on the river.

(Reach Indian Maiden Falls on Counselman Run by walking south past the museum to where the road hairpins right. A rough trail heads left past a boatyard and mobile home park, hugging the riverbank to reach the falls in .75 mile. An easier route is to continue along the road uphill past the hairpin curve. The road bends left, then right, and left again to another hairpin curve to the right. On the curve, a trail leads southeast away from the road to the falls in .8 mile.)

Recent logging has obliterated the trail beyond the little unnamed falls; I was told, however, that when logging is complete, the trail will be rebuilt or relocated so that a circuit will again be possible. Despite the current confusion, don't cross this area off your hiking list. Urey Lookout and Otter Creek alone make a beautiful trip for little effort, and the trail damage here may already be repaired. If you cannot continue, turn back at the falls to retrace your steps past the museum, up the shoreline to your car.

(If you are able to hike beyond the falls, you eventually reach PA 425, bearing north .25 mile beyond PA 425. The trail soon parallels Furnace Run, ending at Split Rock (1 mile past PA 425), where Furnace Run flows into Sawmill Run. Turn right and in .5 mile arrive at the Susquehanna on PA 425. Turn left to find your car in .3 mile.)

20

Coal Lands

Total distance: 5.5 miles
Hiking time: 3 hours
Vertical rise: 500 feet
Maps: USGS 7½' Tower City, USGS 7½' Lykens

The unusual circuit hike north of Harrisburg in Dauphin County takes you to two abandoned railroad tunnels—the Williamstown tunnel and the Big Lick tunnel—connected by State Game Lands 264. The land itself, grass covered but barren like western prairies, was a strip mine in the nineteenth and early twentieth centuries. The old coal mine pits have been filled in and planted with small pines. But the signs of once devastated land are unmistakable: stunted vegetation, hard footpounding soil, and exposed rocky mounds.

To reach the trailhead in Williamstown, take I-81 northeast from Harrisburg 36 miles to US 209, exit 33. Drive US 209 west 7 miles to the Williamstown Road on the right, west of Tower City. Just before Williamstown pass two cemeteries on the right; turn right (north) at the second street beyond the second cemetery's driveway. Park where the street ends at a **T** in 1 block. (For alternate parking, shortening the hike .5 mile, turn north at the fourth street past the cemetery driveway— the intersection of Market and Ray streets—and drive 3 blocks to the paved game lands road.) From Sunbury drive PA 147 to Millersburg to pick up PA 209 east 14 miles to Lykens. Turn left on the Williamstown Road, driving east to the corner of Market and Ray streets. Turn left to reach the game lands road, or continue 2 more blocks for the left to the **T** parking area.

To begin your hike at the deadend in Williamstown, head north along the dirt road that looks like a driveway, beside a white fence. When the trail splits almost immediately, bear right (northwest) through tall oaks with low underbrush, on the widest of many hunting trails through here. Angle left (west) at .3 mile and at .5 mile reach the game lands hard road, .25 mile north of the alternate parking area.

Ahead is the old mine dump where refuse rock from the strip mining process was discarded after the coal was culled. The large grass-covered hill, barren of trees and tall grasses, looks unnatural only on close inspection. The hill ends precisely at the road, banking down sharply. Cross the road and climb to the top for a tremendous view south—the ridge of mountains extends in a straight line to the Susquehanna River, then disappears into the blue haze of summer. To the north, heavily forested Big Lick Mountain is only 800 feet away. In summer when foliage is full there is no hint of the abandoned railroad bed, old mining

roads, and trails that crisscross the mountain, most of them on public game lands open to hikers. You should avoid the area during hunting seasons, but a fall Sunday (no hunting on Sundays in Pennsylvania) is a colorful choice for hiking the Coal Lands.

From your vantage point look north to the edge of the woods where there are several houses. This is your destination, where you will find the abandoned Williamstown railroad tunnel entrance at woods edge. When you reach the houses at 1 mile, turn left on the paved road, rounding it to the right past a two-story red-shingled house. Beyond the house the road (dirt now) bends left again, slightly uphill for .1 mile.

No specific landmark pinpoints the tunnel entrance. I began to notice large pieces of concrete, and finally a faint trail to the right through concrete rubble off the two-track road. I turned onto this trail and felt a blast of cold air almost immediately. The low concrete arch of the tunnel was still 50 feet away, hidden by dense foliage, but the cold draft on a hot, humid summer day was a certain clue. Walk back into the mountain, through debris left from railroading days, 50 feet to where the tunnel is blocked for safety. The temperature is very likely the constant fifty-two degrees found in natural caves. The railroad tunneled through Big Lick Mountain to come out 1 mile north near Rausch Creek in the valley between Big Lick and Bear mountains. The Williamstown tunnel operated from 1850 to 1914, hand-in-hand with coal companies who depended upon the railroad to transport coal out of the mountains.

Retrace your steps from the tunnel back to the main trail. Turn right (west), for a 2-mile walk through scrub pines and small oaks, with occasional views south to the grassy mine dump. Monkey vines entwine the trees, more like jungle than forest. Limestones and slag mining refuse line the forest floor. At the forest edge small pines have gained a foothold in soil that doesn't look rich even where it appears undisturbed. Rotting leaves covering the scoured ground will eventually form a good soil base.

The trail continues west up the mountain where the forest is in better shape. Small songbirds, squirrels, and chipmunks noisily make their presence known and deer tracks cross the two-track. Gradations in the forest floor, bumpy mounds 10 feet in diameter, are piles of mine waste covered with a thin layer of soil. Uncovered heaps of stony refuse make the going rough if you leave the road.

At 3 miles turn sharply left (southeast) downhill at a trail intersection. Turn right in .1 mile, bypassing a trail on the right in another .1 mile. In .1 mile your road ends

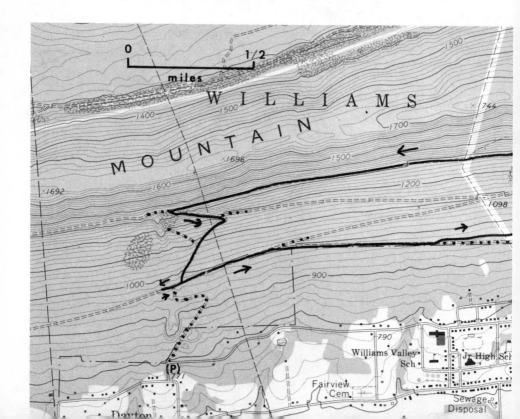

at an old railroad bed without ties; turn right for .1 mile of flat, easy walking to the Big Lick tunnel on the right at 3.4 miles.

The Big Lick tunnel has the same concrete arch—and blast of cold air near the entrance—as the Williamstown tunnel. The two operated concurrently, but the northern entrance of this tunnel through Big Lick Mountain is not indicated on area maps. For a shorter, one-way hike you could spot a second car south of here, at Dayton. Head back the way you came several hundred feet east of the tunnel entrance to a road on the right (south), which reaches Dayton (1 mile west of Williamstown) in .5 mile. For now continue east, bypassing the road you took off the mountain on the left. The level railroad bed angles northeast toward the vicinity of the Williamstown Tunnel.

At 3.8 miles watch for a road on the right, fainter than the railroad bed. Turn and continue east downhill until you reach the open grassy area again. I left the road here to explore the reclaimed land more closely. Although grass covered, the series of hills looks different from a large meadow or field at the base of a mountain. The ground is hard, filled with small rocks tightly packed—I found it impossible to dig a hole in the dirt. Even with a very well broken-in pair of boots it felt like walking on concrete carrying a heavy pack, and my feet hurt before I finished the hike. There were no sticks or branches around—the land was barren of all but short grass no higher than 2 to 3 inches. Erosion in small gulleys showed how easily the thin soil washes away from bare rock. The area reminded me of the Badlands in North Dakota—without cactus.

Continue east to reach the hard road you followed in at 5 miles. Cross the road, still eastbound, to retrace the .5 mile on the dirt road to your car at the **T** in Williamstown. You can also turn right here on the paved road downhill to the parking area at the end of the game lands road. Or, return to the **T** from this alternate parking area by turning left and walking 2 blocks east on the wide dirt road.

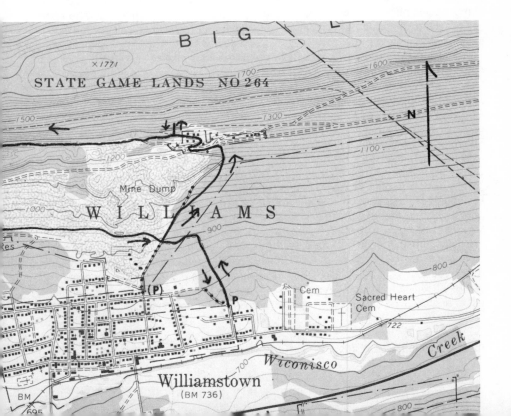

21

Minnich Hit Spring

Total distance: 3.9 miles
Hiking time: 2 hours
Vertical rise: 450 feet
Maps: USGS 7½' Lykens; state forest map

This beautiful area north of Harrisburg atop Broad Mountain near Lykens doesn't get many visitors out of hunting and fishing seasons. Once you've driven here you'll understand why. The dirt road through Haldeman State Forest to the trailhead probably discourages many people, but in good weather when the narrow, potholed road is passable, it's well worth the effort. The quiet remoteness of the mountaintop is extreme—the only sounds are rustling tall pines, rushing streams, and calling birds.

From Harrisburg take US 22-US 322 north to Dauphin, where you join PA 225 to the right. Follow PA 225 for 8 miles, through Powells Valley and Matamoras to PA 147 south of Halifax. Turn right and drive 9 miles east through the valley, past Enterline to Carsonville. In Carsonville the road bears left, then right, reaching White Oak Road in 1 mile. Turn left onto the narrow dirt road uphill, reaching Minnich Hit Picnic Area and parking space on the right in 3 miles. From I-81 take exit 33 to US 209, heading west 16 miles to Lykens. In Lykens turn left on the only road south, driving 5 miles to Lykens Road (dirt) where you turn right. Bear left in 4 miles and reach Minnich Hit Picnic Area on the left in another 1.2 miles.

This circuit hike begins at the picnic area, following dirt White Oak Road northeast, then Lykens Road to an intersection with a woods trail south. (You could start where the trail heads south into the woods from Lykens Road, but the trail is almost impossible to spot from a car and there is no parking.) Leave your car among tall pines at the small picnic area and follow White Oak Road northeast. In 1 mile reach a road intersection and bear right on Lykens Road. (White Oak Road continues to the left 1 mile to a lookout tower and 3 miles to another mountaintop picnic area.) After .3 mile on Lykens Road—also called Matter Road—reach a narrow, unmarked trail on the right. The nearly straight path is visible on both sides of the road when you reach a narrow belt devoid of trees. Hikers, hunters, and snowmobilers sometimes make their own trails in the area, but this is the only straight one that crosses the road.

Turn right off Lykens Road downhill, then uphill on an easy grade. Visibility on either side is good since there are few trees—you'll see just how broad the top of Broad Mountain really is. You are also likely to see (not just hear) grouse among the pines and oaks. Hunting is permitted both in the state forest and in State Game

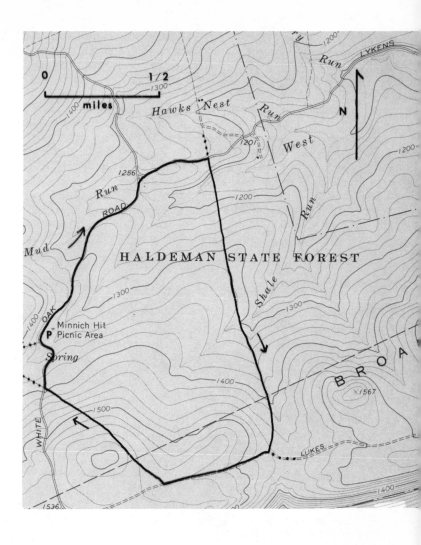

Lands 210 to the east, so Sundays and nonhunting seasons are best for this hike.

In .1 mile cross the West Branch of Rattling Creek, an easy crossing on logs at a low spot even in spring. You'll stay on the straight trail for 1.2 miles, climbing steadily for the first half, then leveling out. At 1.9 miles cross a second stream, smaller and easier than the first. The path gets rocky as it flattens, also causing some hikers to complain that the unmarked trail seems to peter out in fall when leaves cover the ground. Remember that the trail is almost straight, or, as an extra precaution, take a compass bearing where you last were sure of the path and continue on the same heading.

After covering a rocky section of laurel and blueberry underbrush where walking is more comfortable in long pants, you reach Lukes Trail at 2.5 miles. This rocky, wide woods road used by snowmobilers in winter runs east-west through pines and hardwoods with little underbrush.

Squirrels and chipmunks everywhere among the rocks seemed unafraid, perhaps because pine needles underfoot muffled my tread, or because they're not used to human passersby. To the left you'll begin to see the edge of Broad Mountain not far off the two-track. In winter and early spring, a side trip to the edge affords good views of agricultural Powell Valley to the south.

At 3.1 miles turn right onto a broad snowmobile trail, northwest uphill. Walking is carefree on the wide belt of grass and clover, an extension of Grimms Trail, which continues northwest after you leave it for White Oak Road. Snowmobile trails are often excellent hiking—usually wide and less steep than hiking trails, making them more accessible for beginners or hikers not in condition for more severe climbing. Sometimes snowmobile trails cross land that is swampy in summer, or cross streams without bridges, but these are exceptions. If you've explored all the hiking trails near your home, try a snowmobile trail to see some new territory without driving far to find it.

The path pulls uphill, then steadily down to put you back on White Oak Road at 3.6 miles. Turn right and in less than .1 mile pass Minnich Spring, which produces a wide, fairly deep stream. On the left pass the Minnich Hit Trail, arriving at your car at the picnic area at 3.9 miles. The state forest map shows several other trails in the area—Matter Trail, Wolf Pond Trail, Minnich Hit Trail—offering a variety of possible circuits for hikers.

My hiking party wondered about the word *hit* in Minnich Hit Spring, but despite some fanciful interpretations, no one knew the origin of the place name. Further research produced no answers either. One person guessed that *hit* was an old Pennsylvania Dutch word meaning "where the cows crossed over," but given the difficulty of reaching the area, I doubt if there have ever been any cows here. If you know the origin of the term, I'd like to hear from you.

22

DeHart Reservoir

Total distance: 4 miles (approximate)
Hiking time: 2 hours
Vertical rise: minimal
Maps: USGS 7½' Grantville; K.T.A. #4

DeHart Reservoir sits in the valley between Stony and Peters mountains in Dauphin County along wooded PA 325. The area is little visited by passersby, since there are no nearby towns and the nearest homes are about 1 mile away. Built as a water supply for Harrisburg, the lake is closed to boating and camping in most sections. Only hikers, photographers, and other nature lovers are likely to explore here, and you may have the narrow, 4-mile-long lake to yourself.

To reach the trailhead from Harrisburg take US 22—US 322 north along the Susquehanna River 6 miles to Dauphin. Turn right on PA 225, heading north 2.5 miles to PA 325. Turn right, reaching DeHart Dam in 11 miles. Drive another 4 miles to the northeast end of the reservoir, then .7 mile beyond to a small turnoff on the south side of the road near highway mileage marker 10/50. From the northeast take I-81 to US 209, heading west 7 miles to Reinerton. Turn south on PA 325, reaching the trailhead on the left in 9 miles. (If you reach the end of the lake, turn around and approach from the other direction—.7 mile east to the mileage marker and pulloff on the right.)

From Sunbury drive south on US 11—US 15 west of the Susquehanna, crossing on the Clarks Ferry Bridge at Duncannon. Continue south on US 22—US 322 for 1 mile, then turn left on PA 325. In 3 miles you'll join PA 225 south for 2 miles before continuing left (east) toward the dam and lake. No obvious landmarks mark the trailhead. Watch for mileage marker 10/50 on the south side of the heavily wooded road and park in the pulloff.

A worn wooden sign points to a red-blazed trail south that connects with the Appalachian Trail in 4 miles. Both this trail and an unmarked trail south from the parking access reach Clarks Creek at .1 mile. For the rest of the hike you'll be exploring on your own, always within sight of the lake or Clarks Creek. A dead rattlesnake in the middle of the trail before I even reached Clarks Creek was a reminder to be cautious.

When you reach the creek turn right to follow the edge 1 mile to the lake itself. The creek winds and bends, dammed in places by fallen hemlocks creating small pools. Faint fishermen's paths help you find the easiest scramble over rotting logs, which line both sides of the stream. Further west toward the lake, the creekbank gets swampy. Except in the high water of spring melt you shouldn't get wet feet if you're careful. Most of the swamp is on the opposite shore, and where the water extends past the bank on this side, it is only inches deep, with bright green grass piercing the surface.

Walk quietly to avoid frightening wildlife, more abundant in wet areas like this than in woods or mountains. A dozen moulting mallards floated in the creek, unable to fly for the month or so in summer when they are without flight feathers. The males also lose their bright plumage, so that they are nearly indistinguishable from the brown and beige females. The drab colors are camouflage during this vulnerable time, when the birds gather in lake backwaters for further protection.

After .8 mile the creek widens into a swamp where drowned trees provide homes and food for woodpeckers: flickers, red-bellied woodpeckers, and downies. Fish-eating birds scan the territory from skeleton trees while a big-headed, blue and white belted kingfisher sits lookout on a small branch.

Another summer visitor is the American or common egret—a large, graceful bird with a distinctive **S**-shaped neck. The egret was once hunted nearly to extinction because its feathers were fashionable for ladies' hats. The way egrets have repopulated their range is one of conservation's success stories.

At 1 mile the stream and lake meet. A great blue heron sitting quietly in a low branch spotted me, called warning—four squawks—and flew slowly with 6-foot wingspan toward the lake. The stream here has no banks at all, yet the area resembles a badly flooded stream more than a swamp. After a rain, the stream empties muddy water into the lake, defining the stream channel by the difference in water color. The lakeshore is a tangle of underbrush, fallen trees, muddy soil, and swampy growth. If the lake and stream are high you can walk further up the bank to the right, avoiding the tangle along the very edge.

Continue west along the pine- and hemlock-lined lake, on gravel banks when

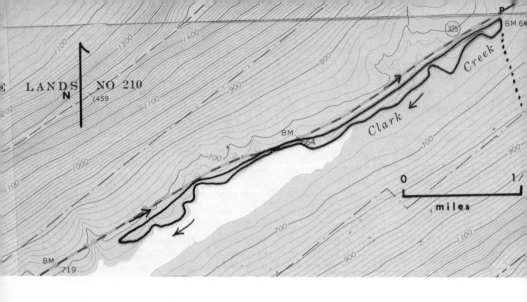

the water is low. Branches and whole trees stranded by lowering water levels litter the banks. Small pools and little inlets, crisscrossed with tracks of raccoon and deer, shelter frogs and tadpoles. At 1.2 miles, where the lake is still very narrow, three does and a fawn splashed into the lake up to their knees. Large rocks jutting into the water offer good vantage points for watching wildlife on the far side of the narrow lake. In spring and fall, flocks of migrating waterfowl all but cover the lake at times.

How far you walk along the lake is really up to you. I turned back where the lake widens, 1.2 miles beyond Clarks Creek, but you could hike all the way to the dam on the southwest end of the 4-mile lake. Return to your car by retracing your steps 2.2 miles back to the trail by the creek, or

walk north about 100 yards, then east for a vastly different return through dense woods just south of PA 325. Tall mature oaks leaving little sunlight for undergrowth alternate with patches of less mature forest—pines with laurels beneath. The straight woods route back is somewhat shorter. At 3.9 miles reach the trail down to Clarks Creek, turn left, and reach your car in less than .1 mile.

DeHart Reservoir is a good place to explore if you don't feel up to the strenuous 8-mile loop that also begins at this parking lot, St. Anthonys Wilderness (see Hike 23). One day when both the heat and humidity suddenly soared above ninety, I chose instead this easy bushwhack without trails, which easily adapts to the hiker's pace and weather conditions.

23

St. Anthonys Wilderness

Total distance: 6.75 miles
Hiking time: 4 hours
Vertical rise: 1,000 feet
Maps: USGS 7½' Grantville, USGS 7½' Lykens

This strenuous circuit northeast of Harrisburg in the largest roadless area in southeastern Pennsylvania is filled with the beauty of the deep woods. Today as remote as any hiking area east of the Susquehanna, St. Anthonys Wilderness (on record as early as 1770) once boasted a stagecoach road and several villages. This hike features a stiff pull up Stony Mountain and a section of the Appalachian Trail (AT) through large hemlocks, pines, oaks, and nineteenth-century ruins. A dead rattlesnake in the parking area increased my caution but lessened the shock of seeing two live ones later on.

Driving access and parking for DeHart Reservoir and St. Anthonys Wilderness are the same. For complete directions see Hike 22. A worn wooden sign at the trailhead points to a trail junction with the AT in 4.1 miles. All mileage calculations are somewhat approximate, but using two different sets of maps, I calculate the distance as 2.6 miles. Although maps and signs don't necessarily keep up with trail relocations, hiking sense says 2.6 miles to the junction is more accurate, and the guide uses that figure.

Begin by heading into the woods downhill on the red-blazed trail to Clarks Creek in .1 mile. Fallen hemlocks provide your bridge across. Large hemlocks and laurels dominate the area here around Clarks Creek, where you turn toward the lake for the DeHart Reservoir hike. For this hike, head south up steep Stony Mountain. The primitive though visible trail is not one you can fall asleep on while walking, but an active, twisting trail that demands concentration.

Begin your climb up Stony Mountain at .3 mile, adding 900 feet of elevation by the old stone tower at 2.2 miles. The most strenuous section comes after 1 mile, climbing 400 feet in roughly .3 mile. Despite the difficulty, I would rate this easier than the ascent to Hawk Rock on the AT near Duncannon (see Hike 25), or the Loyalsock Trail ascent at Canyon Vista (Hike 35).

Before I started this climb, I saw my third rattlesnake. The first live one was near Clarks Creek and this one was heading downhill off the trail. I'd seen copperheads many times around eastern Pennsylvania, but never a live rattler. Further uphill I saw several nonpoisonous snakes for a total of seven, an extraordinarily high number for any hike. I later heard a theory that the driest summer on record was forcing snakes out of their

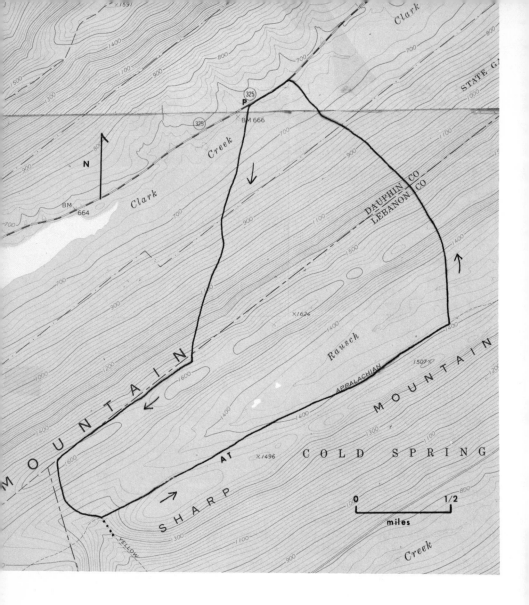

mountain lairs, down to creeks and lakes in search of water. Whatever the explanation, you should be cautious hiking here.

The trail bears right (southwest) at 1.5 miles, and reaches the old stone tower at 2.2 miles. Different sources call this a fire lookout or a remainder from coal mining days. From the tower you can see an old railroad incline plane. The trail turns left (southeast) at the stone tower. Ruins of a stagecoach stopover known as Yellow Springs station remain near here today. Descend 200 feet to reach the junction of the Yellow Springs Trail and the AT at 2.6 miles.

Turn left on the white-blazed AT, climbing 100 feet to the ruined foundations of pre-Civil War Yellow Springs village at 3 miles. To the south below you is the old Schuylkill and Susquehanna Railroad bed through Stony Creek Valley (see Hike 47). (You can reach the railroad by continuing straight ahead on the Yellow Springs Trail instead of turning left onto the AT at 2.6 miles, or from the many side trails down from the ridge.) This hike follows the AT for only 2 miles, but the old stagecoach road you're now on extends 8 miles east of here to Rausch Gap. Beyond where you leave the AT on this hike are the ruins of Cold Springs station and resort.

Today, the stagecoach road leads you right into the heart of St. Anthonys Wilderness, an imposing mountain ridge studded with boulders, tall pines, and magnificent oaks. The land has a wild, unfinished look, although you'll find the old stagecoach line fairly easy walking. You should avoid this area, now part of State Game Lands 211, during fall hunting seasons, except on Sundays when hunting is not permitted.

Elevation changes are minimal until you leave the AT at 4.5 miles to join the unmarked Sandy Spring Trail to the left (north) down the mountain. (If you miss the intersection, which is unlikely, in .25 mile you'll reach well-marked Cold Spring Trail to the right, south.)

The trail descends gradually 100 feet to the stream (part of Stony Creek but known locally as Rausch Creek) at 4.9 miles. Across the stream climb sharply to the top of Stony Mountain at 5.3 miles. From this oak- and pine-forested ridge begin your final descent, losing altitude steadily for .25 mile. A rough and rocky .25-mile section begins at 5.5 miles—the toughest descent of the hike. After 5.8 miles the grade eases, but loose rocks along the trail could send you to the bottom sooner than you wish, if you aren't cautious.

Cross Clarks Creek at 6.3 miles, again on fallen hemlocks. Beyond the creek you reach PA 325 at 6.5 miles. Turn left for the .25-mile return southwest to your car. In late fall 1980, a forest fire swept through a section of Stony Mountain behind DeHart Reservoir, destroying what local officials called "dozens of acres." I rehiked portions of this trail and did not find fire damage. Hikers should be aware, however, that some trails in the area might have been destroyed by that fire—at least temporarily.

Peters Mountain

Total distance: 7.8 miles
Hiking time: 4 hours
Vertical rise: 1,000 feet
Maps: USGS 7½' Duncannon, USGS 7½' Halifax; K.T.A. #4

This circuit hike just north of Harrisburg is rough and steep with easy sections in between. You'll trek up long, lean Peters Mountain on a section of old Appalachian Trail (AT) and return on the new relocation. Stunning views of the Susquehanna River, and wildlife, are major attractions in this wild area where even coyotes and bear are occasionally seen.

To reach Peters Mountain from Harrisburg drive US 22—US 322 north 15 miles to the Clarks Ferry Bridge just north of Duncannon. The Appalachian Trail crosses the Susquehanna on this bridge and immediately heads east up the mountain. Park on the right side of PA 147, just beyond the left turn for those crossing the bridge on US 22—US 322. From the north take US 11—US 15 to the Clarks Ferry Bridge, turn left on US 22—US 322 across the river, then left on PA 147 and park off the road to the right. If you approach on the east side of the river on PA 147 heading south, park on the left about 100 yards before reaching US 22—US 322 and the bridge.

An AT sign and white blazes on the bridge clearly mark the trailhead. Begin walking east, across the railroad tracks beside the road, following the blazes steeply uphill. Be careful on the stiff

beginning ascent—nearly 400 feet in .2 mile—as you lean forward using your hands in places. At .1 mile reach a stream where you turn left amid a stand of hemlocks. The grade lessens for .1 mile, skirting the mountain edge with your first views of the Susquehanna.

At .2 mile the former AT, now a blue-blazed side trail, comes in from the left. Turn onto the old woods road along part of the 25-mile ridge of Peters Mountain. Oak woods with a few pines at higher elevations tower over wild raspberries, thistle, monkey vines, and low scrubby trees. Dense undergrowth frequently obscures the river to your left, but occasional glimpses of the Susquehanna and farmland below are outstanding.

At .8 mile cross a power-line cut with wide-open view. Just after I reentered the woods, a hen grouse flew ahead, then ran across the trail into the bushes. This was a grouse's classic broken-wing trick, designed to lure intruders away from her chicks. When I started to move ahead, the hidden bird's crying and fluttering increased, and I suddenly spotted a tiny down-covered chick almost under my boot. Light brown with darker stripes, the chick lay flat on its stomach, camouflaged

as a pebble hidden in short grass. When I knelt down for a closer look I could see a second and third chick less than a foot away. After several pictures I left the chicks to the care of their worried mother, treading cautiously in case others were nearby.

Climb slightly to an open glade and seasonal stream at 1.25 miles. In one large puddle were hundreds of tadpoles: one-quarter were large bullfrogs, three times the size of the more numerous spring peepers. None had yet developed hind legs and it was unlikely any would live that long. Ringed with drying mud, the puddle was rapidly shrinking. Just as

deadly, the pool had been visited by raccoons who make easy prey of the trapped swimmers.

At 1.8 miles pass another pipeline cut and view of the Susquehanna and farmlands upriver. The old woods road through tall oaks and a few tulip poplars is grass covered and provides easy footing. At 2.8 miles you'll reach a power-line cut and a campfire circle of blackened stones. To the left is a good view of the opposite river bank. Turn right to follow the cut east across a flat, sometimes muddy area. At 3 miles begin a steep, slippery climb—550 feet in .4 mile—toward the radio tower on the crest.

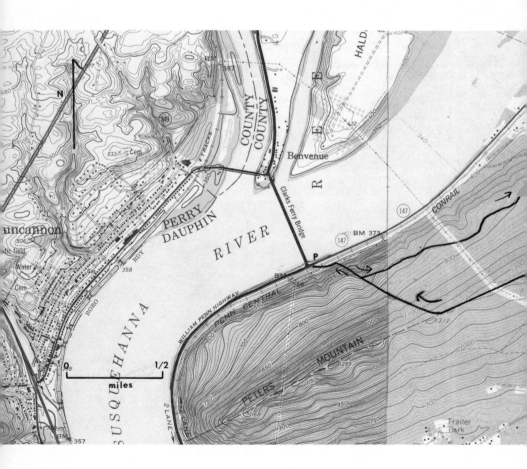

At 3.9 miles you leave the power line to return to the AT just before reaching the tower. Watch carefully for white blazes on rocks and the narrow path to the right; the power-line cut continues straight ahead.

Turn right on the AT to follow the ridge of Peters Mountain back toward the Clarks Ferry Bridge. The ridge narrows toward the river, lightly peppered with Pennsylvania limestones. A common plant is the may-apple, which unfolds a single, white-petaled flower in the notch below two large leaves in April. I have never found the edible lemonlike fruit fully ripened. Sought by nearly all birds and animals, the berries are usually harvested in May before they are totally ripe.

At 5.9 miles cross a pipeline swath for a breathtaking view of the confluence of the Susquehanna and Juniata rivers. You're now 600 feet higher than when you crossed this cut before on the blue-blazed trail, so views are more impressive. In the middle of the river near large Haldeman Island is the much smaller West Fall Island. The rich bottom lands of the islands and mainland support large farms that stretch off to the horizon, bounded by Cove Mountain across the Susquehanna, and Dividing Ridge, Berry, and Mahantango mountains on this side.

Rocks get progressively larger and

more numerous until you head off the mountain. Soon you're winding through car-sized limestone boulders. The darker "greybacks" are sandstone, pried loose from their original locations by frost action and inched downhill over the centuries.

Near the end of the ridge a 5-foot blacksnake, as thick as my forearm, stretched across the path. Black snakes are not poisonous but can be dangerous when aroused. An old woodsman's tale claims that a black snake scares off poisonous snakes for miles around. Don't believe it; there are many cases to the contrary. High rocks to the left and the sheer dropoff on the right meant the snake had to move before I could. When I touched it with a stick, the snake climbed straight up the main branch of a 4-foot laurel beside the trail.

At 7 miles the AT turns right onto a woods road, bearing left in 100 yards. In .2 mile the trail turns right, heading more severely downhill on slippery loose pebbles. At 7.4 miles you'll reach a trail shelter; at 7.5 miles the blue-blazed trail intersects on the right. Follow the white blazes .2 mile back to your car at the bottom of the hill.

Peters Mountain is not for novices. Sections are rough and the hike can easily take most of the day, adding lunch and rest stops. Midsummer is not the best season to hike here: dense vegetation holds in the heat of the day, and interferes with river views. On a warm day in May some areas were like a greenhouse, with temperatures ten to fifteen degrees higher than in the open. Since there is no reliable source of water, you should bring your own.

Susquehanna
West

25

Hawk Rock

Total distance: 7.6 miles
Hiking time: 4¼ hours
Vertical rise; 1,100 feet
Maps: USGS 7½' Duncannon, USGS 7½'
Wertzville; P.A.T.C. #1

Don't confuse this hike with famous Hawk Mountain Sanctuary (see Hike 14) north of Reading, or with a Sunday afternoon walk. This loop hike just across the Susquehanna River from Peters Mountain (see Hike 24) climbs 900 feet in just under 1 mile, clings to a narrow path on the precipitous edge of Cove Mountain, and crosses a sheer rock slide. Compensating for your effort are the grand views from Hawk Rock and the ridge of Cove Mountain. You'll see hawks even if you don't hike in the fall migratory season, and you may meet some end-to-enders on the Appalachian Trail (AT). This hike is not for novices, and you should be in good physical condition.

To reach the trailhead near Duncannon in Perry County, drive north from Harrisburg on US 11—US 15 for 16 miles. Exit left at Duncannon and drive south through town 1 mile to Sherman Creek. Follow the white blazes of the AT across the bridge then right, into an alley that veers sharply right and then left .2 mile to end at a gate where you can park. From the north and northeast take I-81 across the Susquehanna to pick up US 11—US 15, 12 miles south of Duncannon. From York drive I-83 north to the intersection

with US 11—US 15, 19 miles south of Duncannon.

Begin hiking south on the AT, 100 yards beyond the gate; then head left and uphill. Cove Mountain seems to spring from the earth—one moment you're walking on the flat, the next you're scrambling up a steep and rocky incline. By .2 mile the trail is switchbacking up the mountain, and you can expect worse. Cove Mountain looms high above you on the left, but you aren't yet able to see the rocky prominence of Hawk Rock.

You must be surefooted as you climb—a sheer dropoff on the right awaits anyone who missteps. A walking stick increases your balance over the some-times precariously positioned loose rocks lining the narrow path. Avoid this hike when the rocks are wet and slippery. By June, the month the majority of through hikers on the Appalachian Trail reach Hawk Rock, they have logged just over 1,000 miles. End-to-enders who begin north on the arduous 2,054-mile AT at Spring Mountain, Georgia, around April 1 do not climb this stretch on the northeast side of the east end of Cove Mountain. But I always wonder how Grandma Gatewood, the legendary septuagenarian who hiked the AT three times after her seventieth birthday, managed this dizzying and slippery descent.

At .6 mile you reach a wide rock slide extending .2 mile. Look for AT blazes on rocks, and the ever-so-faint leveling of the 12-inch trail through softball-sized rocks. Use extra caution here—the rocks are not embedded in dirt and move very easily. Once past the slide at .8 mile, continue straight ahead on the AT.

You soon reach a switchback left up the mountain. The trail is so steep that you can almost touch the side of the mountain by extending your right hand above your head. The narrow path, with no room for error on the left, snakes precipitously up the mountain with few places to rest comfortably. Near the top where the path veers slightly away from the mountain's edgeline, leave the trail to walk 10 feet to

the edge for the first views north to Sherman Creek and the farmlands beyond. About 150 yards from the crest you begin to see the huge stone promontory Hawk Rock ahead of you. To the left Sherman Creek winds through the valley between Cove Mountain and forested Pine Ridge.

Reach the top of Cove Mountain (elevation over 1,200 feet) at 1 mile—a rapid ascent from just over 300 feet above sea level at the base of the mountain. Straight ahead east and northeast the mile-wide Susquehanna bends to the west just below the Clarks Ferry bridge. Stretching out slightly left, Duncannon hugs the riverbank between the river and surrounding hills.

In early spring, a warm southern wind blowing gently on the promontory brought a mature red-tailed hawk, winging

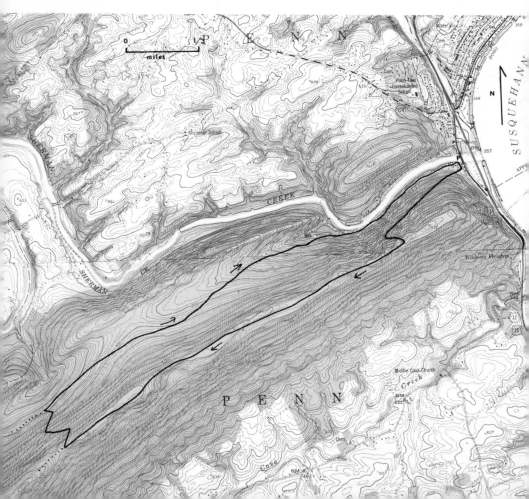

determinedly northward at an elevation that indicated it was migratory. Common in eastern Pennsylvania, these large (wingspan 4 feet), impressive birds are soaring hawks, circling overhead before dropping onto prey in a steep dive. In a half hour I also saw the less common, slightly smaller red-shouldered hawk, and a merlin or pigeon hawk—really a falcon—distinguished from hawks by its steady flapping with strong wingbeats.

Turn right to head back along the ridge of Cove Mountain. From this point elevation gains will be minor, and the sparse ridge vegetation—small oaks, beeches, and hickories 6 to 8 inches in diameter—will not slow your pace. If you leave the path to check for views, you'll notice instead how steeply the mountain falls away from the narrow ridge—hardly more than 100 yards wide. Where the Susquehanna cuts through the mountains, narrow ridges are the norm, but this same ridge even 10 miles west of here is much broader.

At 2.6 miles pass a sign to the Thelma Marks shelter on the left. Although the steep several hundred yards down to the shelter can be difficult for tired hikers, the location offers protection from lightning and gusty winds on the ridge. Water is available several hundred yards further downhill from the shelter.

At 3.6 miles a small, indistinct sign points out an unnamed path on the right. Watch for it where rock outcroppings are fewer and the path slopes gently downhill toward a stand of oaks and hickories. Turn right on to the path, leaving the AT to head off the mountain on a mile-long series of switchbacks down a sharp grade less severe than the earlier climb. The path is faint for the first 100 feet but clearly visible ahead—in places hardly more than a rocky wash. In .25 mile the top of the mountain rises far above you, and the angle eases. Rocks exposed by hikers' boots and running water from small springs help you sight the path down the leaf-covered forest floor.

The trail ends at 4.6 miles on a dirt woods road—turn right and follow the road back to your car. (A left turn would take you to Grier Point, an intersection of several old woods roads.) Surrounded by hemlocks, Sherman Creek parallels the road to the left, 50 to 200 yards away. After walking 1 mile along the creek bed you'll notice logging activity: the road is wider, deeply rutted in places, and intersected by side roads. Keep heading northeast through dense forest, passing a town water storage facility at 6 miles, to where the road ends at the gate and your car.

26

Deans Gap

Total distance: 5.6 miles
Hiking time: 2¾ hours
Vertical rise: 650 feet
Maps: USGS 7½' Wertzville, USGS 7½' Shermans Dale

On a clear day, spectacular views of the Cumberland Valley, and what the Indians called the Endless Mountains of the Appalachians, distinguish this hike west of the Susquehanna River between Harrisburg and Carlisle. Alternately an easy walk and a stiff climb, this circuit links part of the Appalachian Trail (AT) to a section of the old AT and the Tuscarora Trail. Walking the ridge of Blue Mountain is a hike for all seasons—including winter ski-touring and snowshoeing.

The trailhead is 9 miles northwest of Mechanicsburg, just south of the ridge of Blue Mountain that divides Cumberland and Perry counties. From Carlisle or Harrisburg take I-81 to the Mechanicsburg-Wertzville exit. Turn north on PA 114 and reach PA 944 at Wertzville in less than 1 mile. Turn left and continue 2.2 miles to the top of a hill where Appalachian Trail signs mark the intersection of Deer Lane. This is where hikers return to the mountains after a 15-mile road walk through the Cumberland Valley from White Rock (see Hike 27) to Deans Gap. Turn right on Deer Lane and drive back along the potholed dirt road as far as possible. Once past the "No Parking" signs and the few houses, you can park anywhere you can pull off the

road on dry ground. The lane stays muddy long after a rain, and getting stuck here is much easier than getting out.

Begin hiking north on Deer Lane. If you've been able to drive back 1 mile, in a few tenths mile bear left on the jeep road that comes in from the right, following white AT blazes. As you start to climb Blue Mountain, you'll be dodging a seasonal stream that runs in all but the driest weather. Soon the road turns sharply right upward, leaving the stream behind.

As you climb higher on the steep but wide and grassy trail, magnificent views of the Cumberland Valley open up, a welcome sight to through hikers on the AT. The valley cuts between mountain ridges, ending one chain near White Rock south of Carlisle. Hikers on the AT must spend a day walking 15 miles on hard-surfaced roads before reaching the next ridge of mountains to continue through the woods. Although highway hiking is unpleasant for backpackers, the Cumberland Valley is one of the richest agricultural areas in Pennsylvania, and you needn't climb very high before you can overlook the wide expanse of fields extending as far as you can see.

At 1 mile you crest Blue Mountain at Deans Gap; the Darlington Trail and the

AT run to the right, the Tuscarora Trail to the left. A challenging trail for long-distance packers, the Tuscarora runs west and south 105 miles to continue as the Big Blue Trail in Maryland, West Virginia, and Virginia. The Darlington Trail covers 25 miles, separated by the Susquehanna Trail, ending at an intersection with the Horseshoe Trail at Manada Gap, 13 miles east of the Susquehanna. The AT used to continue straight ahead down Blue Mountain, but has been rerouted to follow the Darlington Trail east briefly before turning north to Cove Mountain.

For this hike, continue ahead on the old AT on dirt Deans Gap Road. In 100 feet pass the Darlington Shelter of native limestone. The road descends gradually to Myers Gap at 2 miles, where you turn left on a recently paved road that winds up the mountain. At 2.6 miles you'll cross a power-line cut. This is a short, steeper detour that shortens the road walk if you turn left to follow the cut up the mountain.

Continue on the road to reach Sterrets Gap at 3 miles. Just before reaching PA 34, the road bends sharply right. Turn left here, near a long gravel driveway, and follow the orange-blazed Tuscarora Trail east. From here it is a pleasant 1.5 miles back to Deans Gap atop the single, narrow mountain ridge. Most of the mountains beyond Blue Mountain are

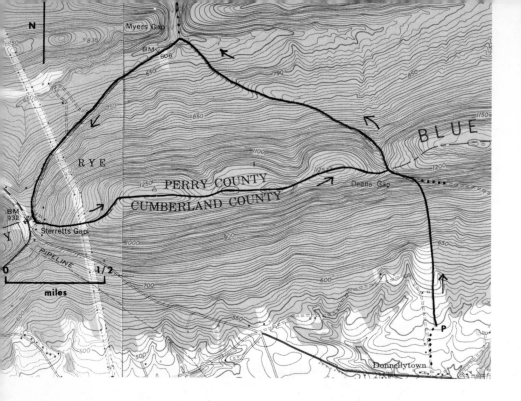

both taller and broader, progressively, as the chain runs northward, or are made of several ridges.

In .2 mile cross the power-line cut again. The swath at first seems an intrusion into the remoteness of the mountain and your hike, but it has compensations. Wildlife, especially deer, frequent the grassy area to feed and browse, and the cut opens a breathtaking view of the mountains to the north and west. Walk out to the edge of the power-line cut on the left for a panorama nearly as wide as that earlier of the Cumberland Valley to the south. Here, there are more mountain ridges—they do seem to go on forever—and only a narrow band of farmland. Fall brings brilliant orange, red, and gold to the hard-wood-covered hills—here we find good-sized oaks, hickories, and a few elms, blighted as elsewhere.

Back on the trail you'll find the way occasionally damp at first. The ridge to the right is rocky, covered in spring with a dusting of spring-beauties. Turkeys and deer are common here, and you'll likely hear the drumbeats of grouse and the "Bob-white" call of quail. When you reach Deans Gap again, watch for white AT blazes and turn right to retrace your steps to your car.

The section along the Tuscarora Trail would be especially good for cross-country skiing or snowshoeing. You could begin at Sterrets Gap on PA 34 and ski eastward to Deans Gap, meandering along the mountain ridge. If you don't mind a strong downhill section, you could also ski from Deans Gap to the hard road. You might ski the section from Deer Lane to Deans Gap, but I wouldn't advise skiing the reverse steep and twisting downhill from Deans Gap to Deer Lane.

27

White Rock

Total distance: 4.5 miles
Hiking time: 2½ hours
Vertical rise: 600 feet
Maps: USGS 7½' Mechanicsburg, USGS 7½' Dillsburg

This short hike southwest of Harrisburg in Cumberland County is tougher than you might expect. The vertical rise is all in one steep climb, and once atop White Rock ridge you'll be scrambling over boulders. Views of the Appalachians and Cumberland Valley from the ridge are far-reaching; closer at hand, you must watch carefully for copperheads, black, and pine snakes in warm weather. This hike avoids technical climbing, but you may see rock climbers in full gear along the rocky ridge wall.

Reach the trailhead by driving US 15 south from Harrisburg 15 miles. Just before Dillsburg turn right (north) on PA 74 and continue 4 miles to Brandtsville. After the railroad tracks (but before the bridge over Yellow Breeches Creek) turn left onto narrow, paved Creek Road, following the stream 1.7 miles (recrossing the railroad tracks at 1.2 miles). When the road makes a hairpin turn to the right around a sycamore that Pennsylvania Appalachian Trail guidebooks call the largest tree on the entire 2,045-mile AT, you've found your parking spot. From Carlisle, take PA 74 south 6.5 miles to Leidigh Road—you'll see AT signs at the intersection. Turn right on Leidigh Road following AT blazes

across the railroad tracks and along the stream 1.5 miles to the old sycamore. If you miss narrow Leidigh Road altogether, stay on PA 74 for 2 miles further to reach Brandtsville and Creek Road.

The venerable sycamore (also called buttonwood) should provide a shady parking place—if the local fishermen who flock to the stream for trout haven't already filled the spaces. Begin hiking on the paved road leading to White Rock Acres, a mountainside housing development, and in .25 mile the AT—your route—leads into the woods on the right, just beyond a farm. Follow the white AT blazes carefully; road building and grading are ongoing here, and the trail has already been relocated several times in as many years. When construction is finally finished the trail can be more permanently established. Be prepared to find that the AT has been relocated here, but the route once you're atop the ridge should be as described.

Follow an old woods road several hundred yards, then turn right onto another, improved, dirt road. By .6 mile you have left the construction for an oak forest with little underbrush except a few laurels and blueberry bushes. Several old clay quarry holes along the way now harbor tadpoles and frogs. Descend slightly before starting the uphill climb, passing a side trail to seasonal Campbell Spring at .9 mile. The AT used to go by the spring, then straight up the mountain, but it has recently been relocated so that you approach at an angle, bear right, and then ascend from a point halfway up the mountain. The rerouted trail is much easier for end-to-enders carrying fifty-pound packs.

Once on top at 1 mile, you'll see why White Rock ridge is so-called. Turn right to follow the AT along the crest. White blazes painted on white boulders (more often than on tree-sized laurels) are tricky to spot at times as they scramble directly over the rocks, rarely around. The boulders slow your pace, allowing you to watch carefully for snakes sunning themselves among the rocks. I saw my first copperhead here—coiled head up, watching me from a waist-high ledge. Copperheads usually leave an area when they hear someone approach, but this one

had no time to escape so it held its ground. The copperhead, with handsome markings of russet and warm brown, is distinguished from the similarly marked milk snake by its triangular head and vertical eye pupils. Watch where you put your feet and hands—not just the ground but also crevices and flat rock ledges 2 to 3 feet high.

Climb out to the top of the boulders along the crest for views left (south) to the endless ridges of the Appalachians, range after range of densely forested mountains. The haze of distance blurs your vision before the mountains end. Right is the Cumberland Valley—once known as Great Valley—where large fields stretch to the next mountain range 15 miles away. Along the .8-mile ridge are sheer rock outcroppings where rock climbers practice for bigger climbs. You may see a group of climbers roped together, one person on top with a belay rope, inching along the 75 feet to the top.

You yourself could almost use technical equipment where the AT blazes head

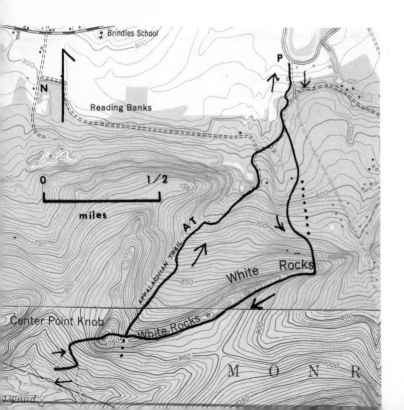

confidently right over the top of precipitous rocks in places. Daunting at first, scrambling up 20 feet only to descend immediately isn't as difficult as it looks. And you'll notice there are always footpaths around the steepest climbs to avoid the rock scrambling.

At 1.5 miles the rocks give way to smoother walking where deer are plentiful. As you near the end of the ridge, tall sweeping pines have gained a foothold among the rocks, whispering in the slightest breeze. At 2 miles the AT heads left down the mountain. Continue straight ahead for 100 yards along the now-faint old AT to the edge of the ridge where a small granite monument commemorates Center Point Knob, once the halfway point of the Appalachian Trail. The midpoint today is somewhere closer to the Susquehanna River, changing slightly each year as the trail is rerouted.

Follow the old footpath another 100 yards for a great vista of the rolling mountains and hollows to the south: Murphy Hill (Cabin Hill), Seven Bench Hill, Pipeline Hill, Colon Hill, and Whiskey Springs Road. The origin of the name Seven Bench Hill is lost to local lore, but I once met a weary backpacker who claimed he needed seven rest benches to get to the top of that steep mountain. One wintry February day I stayed to watch a snow squall come over the mountains, moving closer, hiding ridge after ridge. When I got back to my car there was nearly an inch of new snow down, and I paid for the spectacular sight by a treacherous return trip.

From this point retrace your steps to where the new AT heads off the mountain on the right. Instead of taking the AT, turn left on the faint Old Mine Trail, an old woods road once traveled by mule wagons carrying clay down the mountain. The trail avoids the rocky cliffs and rejoins the AT at 3.8 miles near the base of the mountain. Avoiding the steepness of the ascent, the woodlands road curves downhill past hollows where deer, raccoons, and squirrels gather. In muddy seasons you'll find your hiking boots caked with pounds of heavy, sticky clay.

At 3.2 miles the road comes out onto a wider gravel road. Bear right, and at 3.8 miles rejoin the AT. Turn left to retrace your steps .7 mile down the hill to the buttonwood tree and your car.

Kings Gap

Total distance: 4.1 miles
Hiking time: 1¾ hours
Vertical rise: 700 feet
Maps: USGS 7½' Dickinson; education center map

Ten miles of excellent trails await hikers at Kings Gap Environmental Education Center in Cumberland County southwest of Harrisburg, and more trails are being brushed out and readied. Opened to the public in 1977, the grounds of the magnificent summer home of Frank Masland, owner of Masland Carpets in nearby Carlisle earlier in the century, have been carefully developed for environmental education. Gazing out over the mountains and the Cumberland Valley from the long stone terrace of the mansion is so enjoyable you may forget why you've come. But hiking brings stands of virgin white pine, blueberries in July, and a scenic overlook of the rolling ridges of South Mountain.

To reach Kings Gap from the north, take I-81 south to the PA 34 exit at Carlisle. From the east take the Pennsylvania Turnpike (I-76) to exit 16; then head 3 miles south on US 11 to the PA 34 intersection in Carlisle. Continue 6 miles beyond Carlisle on PA 34. Just after crossing the bridge over Yellow Breeches Creek, turn right (west) toward Huntsdale on a narrow road along the creek. After 5.5 miles a large sign indicates the entrance road to Kings Gap. Turn left to begin the 3.8-mile trip up South Mountain, an extended circling entrance to lessen the grade of the 800-foot climb. Drive slowly and cautiously on this extremely narrow two-way road. At a rock outcrop after 2 miles, a sign cautions you to blow you horn to alert traffic coming down the mountain. When the road splits near the top, turn right and in .1 mile you'll arrive at the imposing stone mansion and parking area.

Built in 1904, the mansion was used by the Masland family as a summer home, and later by Masland Carpets and local civic groups for dinners and parties. Today the mansion houses the environmental center's headquarters, open daily from 8 A.M. to 4 P.M. At the office pick up literature detailing current hiking trails—existing trails may be rerouted in the center's trail expansion program.

Beyond the reception area, the stone terrace at the back looks north and west to the Cumberland Valley and ridges of South Mountain. The hollows between ridges tell an interesting story. This is Kings Gap Hollow, the next one is Irishtown Gap Hollow, followed by State Road Hollow, Kellars Gap Hollow, and Peach Orchard Hollow 6 miles west.

In Pennsylvania, a *gap* is usually a stream cut between mountains. But

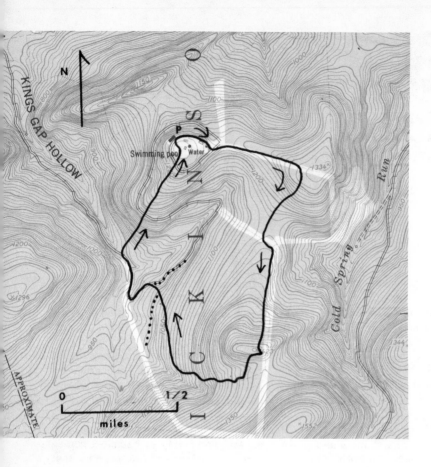

throughout South Mountain, gaps are frequently called *gap hollows*. A *hollow* is normally a depression that does not cut all the way through a mountain. Here, gap hollows are so-called because they are smaller than other gaps in the region, but do extend through much of the mountain, in some places allowing pioneer wagons, or today's traffic, to get to the other side without climbing the mountain. Kings Gap Hollow and others nearby are narrow and gain altitude slowly, winding into the mountains by way of a rocky stream cut.

To begin, return .1 mile down the entrance road to the split where you turned right. Just across the road and slightly left is a small parking lot with a large wooden map at the rear. Begin walking southeast along a fire line on the Scenic Vista Trail, blazed with orange paint circles. Bird houses have been positioned along the 25-yard-wide fire line for small songbirds that like the open, brushy country. At .6 mile turn right across the fire line into the woods.

Pines and hardwoods tower over

knee-high ferns along the broad, flat crest of South Mountain as the trail slopes gradually downhill. At .8 mile bear right at another trail intersection. Stay on the Scenic Vista Trail, passing by brightly-colored mushrooms and fungi. East .5 mile where the ridge falls away to Cold Spring Run, the heavy oaks and pines thin to large mountain laurel. Thick wild blueberry bushes extend for miles, but the thinning oaks block the strong sun needed to nurture berries. At 1.2 miles you'll reach another fire line where blueberries grow in full sunlight, producing ripe fruit in July.

Beyond the fire line reenter thick pine and oak woods, where the trail goes right through the center of three old charcoal hearths—circular earth pits 40 feet across, depressed 3 feet from the forest floor. Here, tightly packed wood was stacked 8 or 9 feet high and burned into charcoal for ironmaking at nearby Pine Grove Furnace (see Hike 49) between the Revolutionary and Civil wars.

At 1.9 miles you reach the promised scenic vista—a stony overlook southeast to the broad, rolling ridges of South Mountain and the range known as the South Mountains. Some cutting of laurels and tall pines is planned to broaden the view. One after another the green, heavily-forested ridges slowly turn blue, obscured by humidity and the damp climate of eastern Pennsylvania.

Beyond the overlook, the trail turns right rapidly downhill, though the grade is not difficult. At the end of the trail, several enclosures—built in 1980 to show the results of deer-grazing—surround patches of forest about 10 feet square. Officials project that in several years these protected areas will be much overgrown, while the surrounding forest remains nearly devoid of underbrush.

The Scenic Vista Trail ends at 2.7 miles on a gravel road; bear right, reaching the paved entrance road in less than .1 mile. Turn left and continue to a small pond and a huge white pine—at least 200 years old according to a sign. The road here parallels a small stream on the left. At 3.1 miles, where the road curves left, a wooden trail post marks the right turn onto Kings Gap Hollow Trail climbing out of the hollow. You'll probably be puffing before you reach the top in .9 mile. You will cross the paved entrance road twice before coming out behind the mansion at the top of the rise. The woods of oak and hemlock dominated by soft-needled white pine must have missed extensive nineteenth-century logging because of the steep grades and difficult access.

Kings Gap Hollow Trail ends after you cross the hard road a second time. Walk straight ahead .1 mile to the mansion; after 100 yards the woods end and you bear left into an open area, past an old brick water tower on the right. Cross the large yard to arrive at the mansion entrance and your car.

Pole Steeple

Total distance: 2.5 miles
Hiking time: 2 hours
Vertical rise: 800 feet
Maps: USGS 7½' Dickinson; state forest map

Pole Steeple on Piney Mountain north of Gettysburg near Laurel Lake is a favorite spot for local adventurers. Don't let the low mileage fool you—this hike is not for people who've never hiked before, nor for the faint-hearted. In fact, if you're a rock climber you could tackle the sheer rock face of Pole Steeple with technical gear. This hike involves climbing the safer center path of scree (loose rocks), climaxed by a short hand-over-hand climb to the top. If you're considering serious climbing, this might be a place to find out if you're really cut out for the sport.

Approach Pole Steeple, in Michaux State Forest in Cumberland County, from Carlisle (west of Harrisburg) via PA 34. From I-81, exit on PA 34 just south of Carlisle. From I-76 (the Pennsylvania Turnpike) take exit 16 and drive US 11 south into Carlisle, turning south again on PA 34. Drive 7 miles south from Carlisle to Mount Holly Springs; .5 mile beyond follow PA 34 right. In 3 miles turn right again, toward Caledonia, at the Twirly Top ice cream drive-in. After 3.5 miles on hard-surfaced Hunters Run Road, turn left on the narrow paved road that runs southwest below Laurel Lake and dam. Park near the turnoff where available. From York take US 30 west to PA 234, just

beyond the city limits. Continue on PA 234 west 23 miles to PA 34 where you turn right (north). Follow PA 34 for 10 miles to the crossroads near Hunters Run. Turn left at the ice cream stand and follow the rest of the driving instructions.

Start hiking southwest on the paved road past summer cottages for .2 mile. Watch for a trail sign to Pole Steeple and the well-worn path to the left. The beginning of the trail seems innocuous, although it heads uphill at a strong rate. But every step seems steeper than the last and in .1 mile, you reach the elevation grade that climbs 500 feet in .5 mile—to top Pole Steeple at .8 mile. The mountain path is thickly forested with oak and patches of pine. If you hike in the morning you should see white tail deer. Turkeys are more often heard than seen.

The lower section, though steep, seems much like any other hike until, almost without warning, the trees end at .7 mile. You look up, and there is Pole Steeple. From the bottom the climb looks impressive, but possible. There are two sides to the sheer, blocky outcropping; between is the long fall of scree—tiny pieces of rock eroded from the main outcropping. Rock climbers attack the face from either side, climbing

hand-over-hand, nearly straight up the boulders. If you have left your pitons and ropes behind, the center pile of scree is your path to the top.

The scree is slippery and the grade steeper than it appears from the bottom of the climb. Solid footwear is especially important for safety on this hike; do not attempt it in sneakers. If you are hiking in a group, don't climb directly behind someone. The scree is loose enough to send small slides down the incline behind you, and anyone following is likely to get stung by the chips.

The difficulty for hikers without rock-climbing experience comes when the 75 feet of scree end almost, but not quite, at the top. For not more than 20 feet you will climb hand-over-hand over chunky boulders until you reach the safety of the top. The squarish boulders are like building blocks, with wide ledges and plenty of room to maneuver. The climb requires more than usual caution, but I would say it is dangerous only for those who are not careful, or those who scare easily looking down.

You reach the top of Pole Steeple at .8 mile, rewarded with exceptional views of the mountains to the north. Beyond Laurel Lake lies the long, convoluted ridge of South Mountain (see Hike 28). On a clear fall day, colored leaves frame your vista with gold, orange, and red. Some people wait until the leaves are off the trees for an even wider panorama. A winter precaution: don't hike when the rocks are ice covered.

Leave Pole Steeple by any of several faint, narrow footpaths to the southeast. Once across the small flat area atop the mountain, head southeast downhill. At .9 mile cross a small spring or seasonal stream where ferns and frogs share space in the wet soil. Jump across and continue southeast, now uphill. At 1.1 miles the

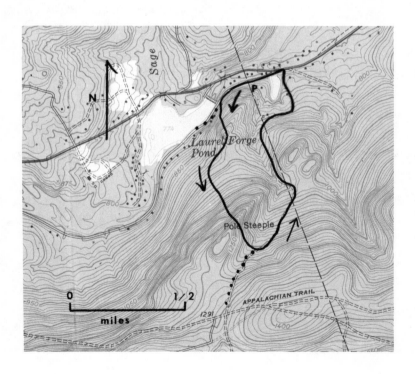

path reaches an old woods road that circles the mountain. Any of the paths south or east from Pole Steeple will intersect the road, but you'll reach it most quickly bearing southeast from the overlook.

Turn left (east and northeast) on a downhill grade for the rest of the hike. The road isn't much as woods roads go—in places hardly more than a wash for spring rains. Farther down the mountain the road widens and the walking eases. At 1.3 miles you begin to pass small stands of pines and hemlocks just off the road to your left. The trees are usually in tiny, low spits, and in most of the spits you'll find evidence of small springs—sustenance for Jack-in-the-pulpits, skunk cabbage, and violets. You'll hear tree frogs and bullfrogs, turkeys, grouse—and deer crashing away in the haste to escape.

Your path downhill follows generally the contour of the land as it winds through a hollow. Several species of moss grow thickly on either side of the road, along with Indian-pipe—parasitic plants with 3- to 4-inch straight white stalks that bow at the end. Hills rise on both sides of the old road, isolating you from outside noises and protecting the animals that seek quiet here.

At 2 miles the road steepens and becomes more pronounced, though still not passable by auto. The road gets progressively better, eventually reaching the summer cottages. The driveways are sometimes in better shape than the road, and if you're not careful, you'll find yourself on someone's front porch. To avoid confusion, take whatever path heads downhill. By 2.1 miles the road has improved enough to distinguish it easily from the driveways.

At 2.3 miles reach paved Hunters Run Road. Turn left and at 2.4 miles, turn left again onto the road past Laurel Lake, for a .1-mile walk to your car.

30

Tumbling Run

Total distance: 4 miles
Hiking time: 2 hours
Vertical rise: 600 feet
Maps: USGS 7½' Dickinson, USGS 7½' Walnut Bottom;
state forest map

Who could resist cascading waterfalls in a hemlock-filled gorge, spectacular vistas of never-ending mountain ridges, and the taste of wild blueberries? This 4-mile loop 25 miles northwest of Gettysburg and 18 miles southwest of Carlisle offers all of these as you cross privately owned game lands and Michaux State Forest.

To reach the trailhead on the Adams-Cumberland county line, drive US 30 northwest from Gettysburg 15 miles to PA 233 at Caledonia. Turn right (northeast), passing unpaved Dead Woman Hollow Road on your left in 9 miles. The parking area is 1 mile beyond on the left, just before a righthand curve in PA 233. Coming from Gettysburg, pull off the road at a small, white boundary sign—"Cumberland County." (If you reach dirt Woodrow Road on the left, you've gone .5 mile too far.)

From the north take I-81 to PA 34 at Carlisle. Drive south 7 miles, turning right (still on PA 34) just beyond Mount Holly Springs. Just past Hunters Run turn right at an ice cream drive-in and continue to Pine Grove Furnace to pick up PA 233. Park .5 mile beyond Woodrow Road on the right before reaching the white boundary post.

A faded woods road—Dug Hill Road—heads north downhill into the woods from the parking pulloff. In .1 mile reach noisy, rock-filled Mountain Creek. The bridge is no longer here, but you can keep your feet dry by taking a faint path downstream 25 yards to cross on a rickety plank. Except when water is high after spring rains, you can also walk upstream a short distance to a fording point.

Once across rejoin unmarked Dug Hill Road, which parallels Tumbling Run, then heads right in .4 mile—away from the stream. In a small clearing among large oaks turn left on another unmarked trail to the edge of the stream. If you can't find the path, bear left to the stream in 100 yards, and turn right on the Tumbling Run Trail uphill. Paths worn by hikers over the rocks seem to begin and end without warning; keep the stream on your left and continue uphill if in doubt.

Huge hemlocks 5 feet in circumference climb out of the gorge high above other trees. Rocks get larger and the water quickens higher up the gorge. In places, downed trees dam the crystal clear water into deep pools; in others, water tumbles noisily over huge, flattened boulders. Scrambling is now the order of the day, and good boots a must. I don't recommend this hike for children because of the constant supervision needed on the often slippery rocks.

At .9 mile reach 40-foot Tumbling Run Falls. In spring, cascading water makes so much noise you have to shout over the roar. Reaching the top of the falls is the most serious climb of the trip. If you're experienced, you can work your way up the wet and slippery boulders, sprayed by mist from the falls during its spring fullness. To avoid this precarious rock climb requiring handholds, head uphill to your right on one of several steep paths out of the gorge.

The natural Stonehenge-like maze of house-sized boulders at the top of the gorge is known as Lewis the Robber Rocks, reputed to be the hideout of a notorious nineteenth-century bandit. Local legends claim that the haul from an Army payroll wagon heist remains buried in the area today. At the top of the falls leave the now quiet stream to walk 100 feet out toward the rocks for a spectacular view south across tree-covered ridges. The wind has swept and stunted the pines into interesting gnarled shapes just waiting for your camera.

Return to the stream at 1.1 miles and continue north upstream. Many people hike only the 1 mile to the falls or up to Lewis Rocks, so the path here is faint. You may have to jump across several times, but keeping the stream on the left is generally easier. At 1.4 miles look left to the pond and log cabin of the Tumbling Run Game Preserve, privately owned by a group of Carlisle outdoorsmen for hunting. I have hiked Tumbling Run year-round and believe you will have no worries even in hunting seasons. Although not as common in this part of the state as copperheads, rattlesnakes seem to predominate in the stretch from the top of the falls to the cabin.

Cross the stream to join the road left

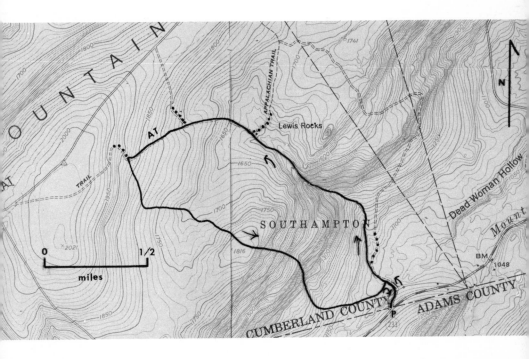

(west) behind the cabin. When the road heads north at 1.8 miles, continue west on a narrow, unmarked trail. (If you miss this turnoff, continue on the road another .4 mile to the Appalachian Trail (AT) intersection and turn left, south.) Hiking shorts will invite scratches from scrub laurel, rhododendron, and dense, stunted oaks on top of the mountain—the aftermath of a forest fire. The laurel blooms in late May, alive with butterflies and bees. Larger animals seem to be visitors rather than residents, but small forest birds—and ants in huge hills—populate the dry ridge.

Reach the white-blazed AT at 2.1 miles, turning left on the old road for an easy .1 mile. At the first intersection (wooden sign), turn left (south) downhill onto the Anna Michener Cabin Trail. In .3 mile reach the log cabin, which may be reserved by writing to the Appalachian Trail Conference for the key. Be on guard for snakes congregated in stacked wood under the porch.

The blue-blazed Blueberry Trail heads south in front of the cabin. In 100 yards a shallow seasonal spring dampens a 25-foot circle, suitable for ferns and frogs but not drinking water. Most of the blueberries are beyond the spring, conveniently waist high for hikers. In a good season, you could easily fill a quart pail in 15 minutes.

In .4 mile reach a rocky overlook where oaks block the best views. The narrow trail heads sharply downhill, then winds left (east) for one lingering vista of mountain ridges framed by high-branching tall pines. In .5 mile cross a grassy bog—springtime green all summer—then left to parallel a branch of Tumbling Run. In .3 mile cross Tumbling Run, turning right on Dug Hill Road to retrace your steps across Mountain Creek .1 mile to your car.

31

Gettysburg

Total distance: 8 miles
Hiking time: 4 hours
Vertical rise: 220 feet
Maps: USGS 7½' Fairfield, USGS 7½' Gettysburg; park map

This 8-mile bridle trail in Gettysburg National Military Park takes you across places remembered from history books: Little Round Top, Seminary Ridge, and Round Top. A quiet walk through woods and fields that saw 51,000 soldiers die will bring you closer to this Civil War conflict than the usual tour on the park's 35 miles of roads. Reminders of those three terrible days in July 1863 are everywhere—from the 1,400 Civil War monuments to the miles of stone walls thrown up hurriedly by both sides against enemy bullets. Stop at the Visitors Center, just south of Gettysburg off Business Route 15, for free information and map of trails in the park's 3,500 acres.

Located in Adams County, Gettysburg is 37 miles south of Harrisburg and 29 miles west of York. Take new US 15 south from Harrisburg, exiting on PA 116 west into Gettysburg's town square. At the traffic circle turn left (south), still on PA 116. In 1 block turn right on PA 116, out of town. At the top of a hill .7 mile beyond the square reach the Lutheran Seminary on the right. Turn left here onto well-marked Confederate Avenue along Seminary Ridge—site of the rebel encampment —and drive .6 mile to McMillan Woods (sign). Park at any of the pull-offs that don't block views of the granite monuments.

Access from eastern Pennsylvania is easiest on US 30 into Gettysburg. Bear right on PA 116 (2 blocks before the traffic circle), then follow the rest of the directions. A more scenic route past the battlefield is Business Route 15—well marked from US 15. You can get on this road as far away as Heidlersburg, 8 miles north of Gettysburg. Follow Business Route 15 into town to PA 134, turn left (south), and continue to PA 116 at the traffic circle.

The trailhead is along the split rail fence on the west side of Confederate Avenue, across from the North Carolina monument. Soldiers seem to spring from the granite of this famous memorial, the first of many monuments commemorating states and positions of fighting units in the battle. Walk south on the narrow bridle trail paralleling Confederate Avenue. Farther on, Gen. Robert E. Lee sits astride his famous horse Traveler—depicted in the granite of the Virginia Memorial.

Marked only at intersections with paved roads, the bridle path weaves in and out of a mature oak forest, skirting the edges of a field, through the site of the battle's heaviest fighting on the second day, July

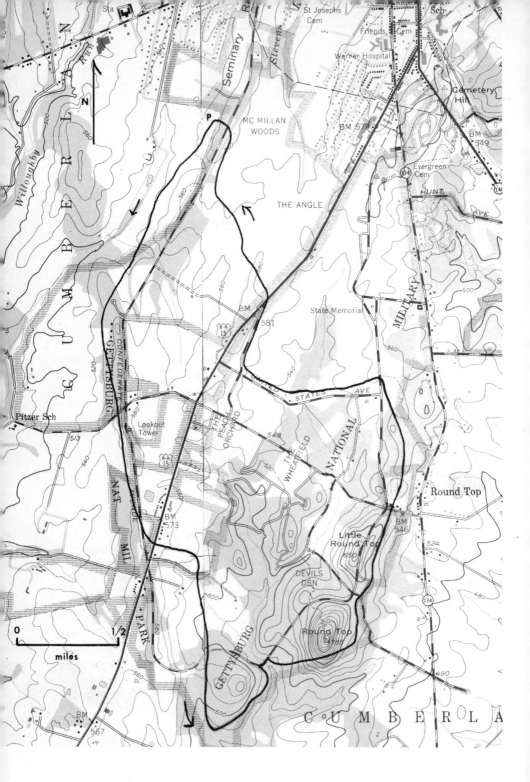

2. By .75 mile you are in view of the Eisenhower National Historic Site on the right. The former war hero and military leader was drawn to the historic American battleground and purchased the 200-year-old house and farm in 1950, slowly renovating it as a gracious home away from the White House. The President spent much time here from his retirement in 1961 until 1969 when he died; Mamie remained 10 more years until her death. Opened to the public in 1980, you can arrange for free tickets to tour the house at the military park Visitors Center.

The trail approaches within 20 yards of Confederate Avenue, past an outdoor auditorium used for church services and presentations by park rangers. In the woods beyond you are likely to see whitetail deer, in small groups or alone in spring and summer. Since hunting is not allowed in the park, the deer herd has grown to troublesome size. In winter when the deer "yard up" and stay in one large herd numbering over 100, they cause considerable damage to shrubs and trees.

After 2 miles the trail turns left across Confederate Avenue, past the tiny whitewashed building where Confederate General Hood directed the second day's preparations. Cross Business Route 15 (Emmitsburg Road) to continue east .2 mile down a dirt lane, then turn right (south) around the edge of a barn of Civil War vintage. For the next .4 mile stone fencerows line both sides of the path, leaving only enough room for horsedrawn wagons. These could have been built by farmers, but many breastworks built hurriedly by both Union and Confederate soldiers remain throughout the park. The low 2-foot walls of native stone are in good condition, covered with honeysuckle and other vines. Towering oaks here are large enough to have weathered the battle.

Recross Confederate Avenue at 2.7 miles. If you walk a short distance left to the first clearing you can see Granite farm. The Spangler farm, overrun during the second day of fighting, has been renamed and restored to its working Civil War state. Admission is free to the farm, which allows no cars; the entrance is .5 mile up the road.

Beyond the hard road are more stone walls and monuments detailing the positions of Union troops. Maj. Gen. George A. Custer's Brigade of the First Michigan was attacked here by Confederates stationed along Seminary Ridge. Huge boulders for cover made it a good fighting spot, but the position was not important and the main assault came at Little Round Top and Devil's Den.

Several more Michigan cavalry monuments are visible only to hikers or horseback riders as the path loops around the ridge back to the road to cross Plum Run by bridge, then back into the woods around Round Top. At 3.5 miles walk through an area where dogwood blooms in May and laurel in June. At 4.1 miles cross another hard road and continue behind Little Round Top. Some of the bloodiest fighting in the war took place west of this ridge at Devil's Den. This was overrun by the Confederates who then assaulted Little Round Top—where they were finally repulsed.

Park officials have recently reconstructed the area to look as it did during the Civil War. Heavily forested for years, the western ridge of Little Round Top has been cleared to its rocky, barren condition after the battle. At 5 miles cross another hard road. To the right a branch of Plum Run tumbles below you, said to have run red with blood during the battle.

At 6 miles turn left across Hancock Avenue to parallel United States Avenue, leaving the forest for the surrounding fields. At the next intersection turn right on the paved road north to Emmitsburg Road at 7.1 miles. Here the connector roads end and the trail becomes difficult to see. Looking northwest you can see your destination, the Virginia and North Carolina monuments and the treeline of McMillan Woods. Cross the road and continue northwest on the faint path through the field—sometimes planted in wheat. At treeline turn right (northeast) and proceed .2 mile. Here the trail swings back to Confederate Avenue and your car.

32

Lake Marburg Trails

Total distance: 4 miles
Hiking time: 2 hours
Vertical rise: 100 feet
Maps: USGS 7½' Hanover; state park map

The bridle trail at Codorus State Park in southern York County southwest of York is longer and more challenging than the park trails designed for hikers. Excellent views of 1,275-acre Lake Marburg, a stroll through a mature pine plantation, and opportunity to observe a variety of woodland and water birds and animals make this a pleasant morning or afternoon outing.

To reach Lake Marburg from York, take US 30 west to PA 116. Turn left (south), drive 9 miles to PA 216, and turn left (southeast) 2 miles east of Hanover. PA 216 takes you, in 1.5 miles, to the western edge of Codorus State Park and Lake Marburg. Before reaching the trailhead you will cross three major bridges over the lake. After Third Bridge, turn left on Sinsheim Road; park in the lot 1,000 feet beyond the intersection on the left. From Gettysburg (see Hike 31), take US 30 east 1 mile to the PA 116 intersection. Head southeast on PA 116 for 11 miles, turning right (southeast) on PA 216, 2 miles east of Hanover, and continue to the parking area.

Begin your hike at the northeast corner of the parking lot, just west of Sinsheim Road. The path is visible immediately as it heads north, then angles west and south, paralleling the uneven shoreline of Lake Marburg. Along the lake's edge, you walk through nearly open fields overgrown with small scrubby saplings. Geese and mallards frequent the coves and inlets of the lake; during fall migration, you could see hundreds or even thousands of geese, as well as bluebills, golden-eyes, buffle-heads, and other waterfowl. Near the edge of the lake, well known to local fisherman for its warm-water species, you may see schools of small bluegills or yellow perch.

At .75 mile the bridle trail loops to the right (southeast) away from the lake, crosses Main Launching Road at 1 mile, and turns northeast. By 1.2 miles you are paralleling Sinsheim Road. Follow the road across Sinsheim Cove on a spit of land, and at 1.5 miles, turn left (northwest) away from Sinsheim Road onto the Ranger Trail. If you've brought a camera, some fine shots are waiting for you along the east shore of Sinsheim Cove. West just offshore is Round Island, a gathering spot for gulls, geese, and other water birds. Further west, slightly beyond good viewing range without binoculars, is Long Island. The lakeshore is well populated with small birds that like the security of the tall grass, multiflora rose, and other scrub growth.

You soon reach the tip of triangular Sand Cove, where the flat trail is easy walking with some minor erosion from horseshoes. At 2.5 miles the trail heads southeast along the park boundary. As you make the right turn, look to your left to see the dam owned and built by the Glatfelter Paper Company of Spring Grove. The impoundment of Codorus Creek created the lake in its backup, named after the small community of Marburg covered by the impoundment. The arrangement is unique in Pennsylvania: the dam is privately owned, and the lake supplies water for the paper company, the town of Spring Grove, and state park recreational facilities.

At 2.75 miles cross Sinsheim Road and continue southeast around the perimeter of a large cultivated field. Soon the trail heads southwest past the backyards of several homes. At 3.2 miles, head slightly downhill through a thicket of brambles to reach a mature forest. In the woods the trail follows a small stream, crossing it

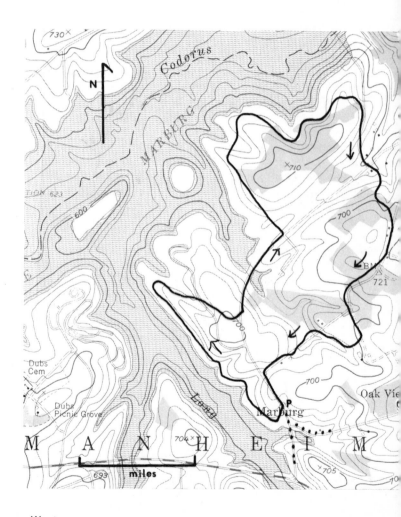

several times. The small inlets of Sinsheim Cove present the only difficulty in hiking the bridle trail. Although none of the crossings are at deep water, the streambanks are quite muddied from horses' hooves. If you go off the trail slightly up or downstream to find your own crossing point, you can avoid getting wet feet. Once past the creeks at 3.5 miles, you can enjoy this attractive forest of tall mature oaks. There are enough good views through the woods to make this section a real treat on crisp fall days when the leaves are changing color.

Beyond the streams climb slightly into a plantation of mature pines on a pleasant and quiet needle-covered pathway between rows. The trail through the pines shows some signs of erosion on the uphill to Sinsheim Road. Turn left (southeast) and follow the road back to the parking lot and your car at 4 miles.

You can extend your hike by taking the 1-mile loop of the Ranger Trail that heads left off Sinsheim Road just beyond the bridge across the inlet near your parking area. The heavy underbrush in this wooded section prevents long views but offers good chances of observing wildlife. In .5 mile you reach a small parking lot on Lakeview Road. To return, find the trail out of the parking lot on your right, a few feet away. Head back northwest, reaching Sinsheim Road at .9 mile, and your car in another .1 mile.

33

Conewago Lake

Total distance: 10 miles
Hiking time: 5 hours
Vertical rise: minimal
Maps: USGS 7½' Wellsville, USGS 7½' Dover;
state park map

Hiking the 10-mile uneven shoreline of Conewago Lake in Gifford Pinchot State Park south of Harrisburg is a challenge not enough people take up. In some sections you will follow established park trails; in others you'll blaze your way through lakeshore undergrowth or find easy walking through oak woods and old fields. In spring the shoreline can be too wet for good hiking, and hunting is allowed in some sections of the park during fall (except on Sunday). A long Sunday afternoon in autumn, or a day on skis or snowshoes in winter, is ideal for observing the beauty of Conewago Lake.

From Harrisburg take US 15 southwest 15 miles to Dillsburg to reach PA 74. Turn left (south) onto PA 74, driving 7 miles to Rossville where you head northeast on PA 177 for .7 mile to a parking lot on the left, just before the first bridge across the lake. From York take PA 74 northwest 15 miles to Rossville, turn right on PA 177, and continue to the parking lot on the lakeshore. From I-76 (the Pennsylvania Turnpike) join US 15 at exit 17, 7 miles north of Dillsburg.

Begin your hike by crossing PA 177, walking southeast down the embankment to the water's edge. Duck hunters set up their decoys in the dense undergrowth of thistles and brambles along the south shore here, and fishermen try their luck where the lake narrows under the bridge. Their comings and goings have established a faint path through the thick tangle at the shoreline, but for the first mile you'll have no better trail. In wet weather you can unexpectedly sink up to your ankles in mud here, but the only really tricky portions of the hike are at this end of the lake—1 mile at the beginning and the last mile of your return.

At .6 mile round an inlet and head northeast. Waterfowl gather along the edges of the lake, preferring the underbrush at the ends of these inlets. Leave the hunting area behind, and at 1 mile you'll be out of the mud and murky undergrowth and entering a deciduous forest where you'll find the Lakeshore Trail. This is fairly wide, well traveled, and parallel to the lake, like other park trails.

Walking around Conewago Lake's uneven shoreline means weaving in and out—around a point and back to circle an inlet—changing scenery drastically sometimes in less than .5 mile. At 1.4 miles you'll reach a bench with a roof where you can comfortably watch the activities on the lake. The Conewago Day Use Area extends from this trail shelter to

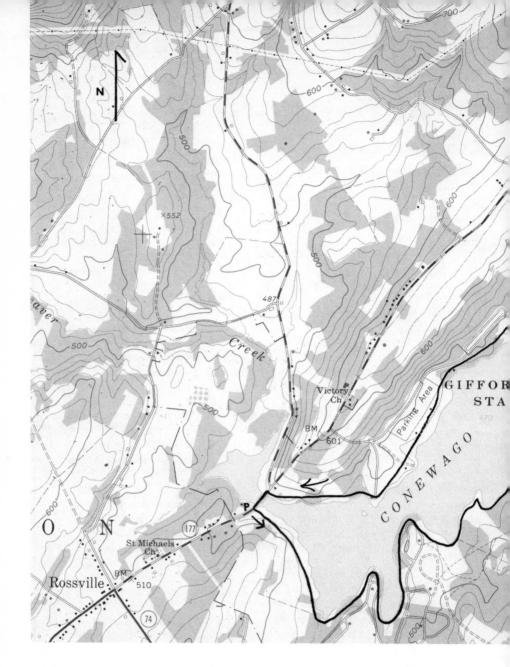

the 3.5-mile point of your hike. Although you can't avoid people in this picnicking and swimming area, the swimmers rarely venture beyond the concession stands.

At 2 miles reach another covered bench on the third point into the lake. Look for a trail that begins where the cut grass ends, leading along the lakeshore into tall oaks among bracken ferns. At 3 miles cross a small stream, dodging rocks on either side. Rocks along the trail grow larger, finally becoming the namesakes of

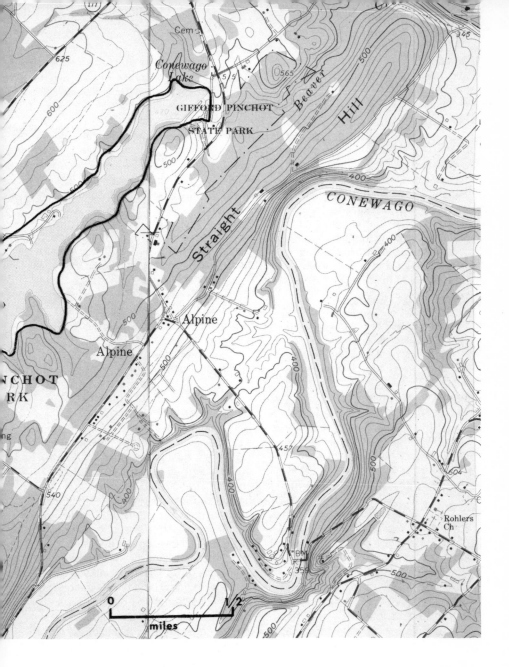

Boulder Point. Frost action on the dark boulders in some places fractured the rock far enough for a person to walk through, or a 4-inch tree to grow between the halves. A large, greyish osprey, also called a fish eagle, scouted the water from a dead tree, dived to the surface, and flew into another tree dangling a small blue-gill from its talons.

At 3.7 miles you'll pass a boat mooring area. The lakeshore is grassy and easy walking even without a trail, although ticks are a problem in spring or early summer. Beyond the mooring area, enter a dry oak forest, spectacular in fall when the oaks turn shades of red and gold. As you continue, you'll cross more and more areas where woods alternate with old fields of tall grass. Man-made Conewago Lake was created by the impoundment of Beaver Creek, flooding the farmland behind the dam. By 5 miles the lake has narrowed, and at 5.5 miles you reach the dam. If you're hiking in a dry season, try crossing at the bottom of the dam along the stream, or, follow a stream from the dam 150 yards out to a hard road, cross the bridge there, then return to the lakeshore.

Continue your circuit on the Quaker Race side of the lake—an unusual name that refers to a straight stretch of PA 177 to the northwest, where Quakers returning from Sunday meeting at Warrington Meeting House are said to have raced their horses. Warrington Meeting House, built in 1769 and still in use in nearly its original condition, was on your right on PA 74 just before reaching Rossville. Keep walking through the cool, pretty woods beyond the dam, and at 6 miles the narrow trail crosses a stream by bridge. In spring you'll find lush wildflowers: wood-sorrel, trillium, and pink lady's-slipper. Never very common, this large, showy orchid has been devastated by unknowing collectors who tried to transplant the flowers to home gardens.

At 6.5 miles the trail and woods end in a broad field. Leave the lakeshore and follow the field southwest, paralleling the lake for good views from hills that were farmland before the valley was inundated. Today, forest regeneration has begun on the edges, but the tall-grass field is still primarily open. Head down the hill when you see a boat mooring area below you on the left. Southwest of the mooring is a service road at 7.1 miles, closed to traffic but good hiking. Farmland wildlife—groundhogs, rabbits, and pheasants—fill the band of woods along the road. A large painted turtle soaked up some sun on a point jutting into the lake, surrounded by two small children and several fishermen. In the center of the old field, park officials have placed wooden bird nests to encourage native birds to set up housekeeping. A bluebird flew from one and a flock of purple martins resided in a small apartment house, among neighboring starlings.

The dirt service road ends at another swimming area parking lot. Walking past the picnic tables and boat rental stand, reach the beach at 8.9 miles. Where the lake begins to narrow, hundreds of Canada geese at a time stop over on their spring and fall migrations. Pass a section of beach for campers to reach the most challenging 1 mile of the hike at 9 miles. The thick trailless undergrowth of brambles and small trees is frequented by mallards and occasional fishermen, though neither have eased the way for hikers. Walking is somewhat easier if you leave the lakeshore even 25 yards. Eventually the tangle ends and you climb the bank to reach PA 177 and the bridge over the western finger of Conewago Lake. Turn left on the hard road and cross the bridge to return to your car on the right.

Northern Tier
and the Pocono
Plateau

34

Glens Natural Area

Total distance: 6.9 miles
Hiking time: 3¼ hours
Vertical rise: 1,000 feet
Maps: USGS 7½' Red Rock; state park map

There can't be many places where, while hiking a 4.5-mile triangle, you can see twenty-two named waterfalls and giant conifers that were growing when Columbus landed in America or William the Conqueror stormed England. Fortunately for eastern Pennsylvania, Ricketts Glen State Park in the Luzerne and Sullivan counties west of Scranton is such a place. You'll hike in along Kitchen Creek through Ricketts Glen to reach the Glens Natural Area—the wedge of land between Ganoga Glen and Glen Leigh gorges—a Registered National Natural Landmark since 1969. You then make a triangular circuit of the gorges spattered with waterfalls, returning through the ancient trees of Ricketts Glen.

To reach this magnificent 13,000-acre park, take I-80 to Benton exit 35. Follow PA 487 north 22 miles to Red Rock, then turn right on PA 118, driving 1.6 miles to the Boston Run Natural Area on the right where you'll find parking, a concession stand, and the trailhead. (To shorten the hike to only the 4.5-mile falls trails, or to camp at the Ricketts Glen State Park campground, you must drive 3 miles north of Red Rock up a tortuous hill on PA 487. Signs warn travelers with trailers *not* to attempt the grade, but to make a nearly

20-mile detour to approach from the north on US 220, then south on PA 487 at Dushore. If you continue north from Red Rock, climb steeply 1.5 miles, reaching the park entrance 3 miles beyond Red Rock. Inside the park, turn right at the park office and drive .7 mile to the Lake Rose parking area where you can begin the 4.5-mile triangle hike of the Ganoga Glen, Glen Leigh, and Highland trails in the Glens Natural Area.)

The longer hike described here begins on the west side of Kitchen Creek near the food concession. Start walking north on the west edge of the creek on an unblazed but well-marked path. Cross Maple Spring Brook at .7 mile (and Kitchen Creek several times before reaching Waters Meet at 1.75 miles.) By 1 mile you've climbed into the heart of Ricketts Glen, named for Col. Robert Ricketts, who helped turn back Pickett's Charge in the Confederacy's unsuccessful assault during the Battle of Gettysburg in 1863. Colonel Ricketts and his heirs controlled over 80,000 acres of land in the area at one time, selling more than half to the Pennsylvania Game Commission in the 1920s. The area was approved as a national park in the 1930s, but World War II ended those plans and the land eventually became state owned.

The glens area is rich in hemlocks, pines, and oaks, many 500 years old and 5 feet in diameter. Rangers have reported fallen trees with as many as 900 annual growth rings. The magnificent trees continue up the stream cut, but they are best seen in this section where they're not so far above the level of the trail.

At 1.3 miles pass Shingle Cabin Brook on the east side of Kitchen Creek. The grade steepens and you see the first named falls, the 16-foot Murray Reynolds, splashing noisily above you. The second is 36-foot Sheldon Reynolds, then 27-foot Harrison Wright just before Waters Meet. From this point on, along both the west and east branches of Kitchen Creek, when you reach the top of one large waterfall, you'll see the next. Most are named for relatives of Colonel Ricketts or for Indian tribes. Although a few are marked with

signs at the base, the state park map showing the name and height of each of the major falls is your best guide for identification.

At 1.75 miles reach Waters Meet, the confluence of the western Ganoga Glen and eastern Glen Leigh branches of Kitchen Creek, and the southern tip of the 4.5-mile Glens Natural Area triangle. Stay on the left (west) side of the creek as you follow the Ganoga Glen Trail northwest toward the Lake Rose parking lot. A series of steps cut into the shale help you climb, continually uphill but not particularly difficult even for novices, if you move slowly. In places the path is quite narrow and usually wet—a dangerous combination where you follow the very edge of the stream cut. Do not attempt the path in sneakers, or if you are not in good health.

The first waterfall in the Ganoga Glen

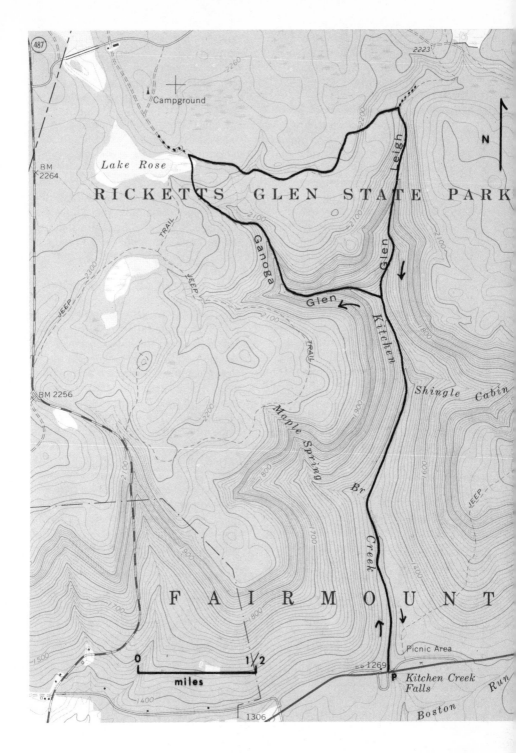

gorge is 47-foot Erie, followed by Tuscarora, Conestoga, Mohican, Delaware, Seneca, the spectacular 94-foot Ganoga, Cayuga, Oneida, and Mohawk—all tribes of the Iroquoix nation—and literally dozens of other unnamed waterfalls. No two falls are even remotely alike, and description could not begin to account for their beauty. At Ganoga Falls a side path to the right leads down to the base of the falls, an excellent place to photograph the entire cascade. Continue ahead on the main trail where another path—very narrow and slippery—heads right, almost into the center of the falls. The main trail turns left up a switchback to reach the very top of Ganoga Falls for a spectacular if dizzying view.

At 3 miles the Ganoga Glen Trail ends at an intersection; left is the Lake Rose parking lot in 200 yards. Turn right on the relatively flat Highland Trail connecting the two gorges, past pines, hemlocks, and large, flat shelves of shale sometimes tossed in many directions, like a giant group of children's blocks. Just shy of halfway is the Midway Crevasse, where huge boulders form an imposing fortress, tumbled into positions that hardly seem natural. The trail reaches the Glen Leigh gorge at 4.3 miles.

It is useless to talk about which branch of the stream is the "best," but I find this eastern section more interesting, even with fewer falls and nothing to rival Ganoga Falls in size. Scrambling down into Glen Leigh you feel more as though you're right among the waterfalls, surrounded on all sides by rock walls and the creek. The descent here is more rigorous than the climb on the other side. The falls themselves have etched deeply into the stream cut, occasionally creating deep rounded bowls of rock into which you descend following the falls path.

I saw a 5-inch trout dart among rocks in the stream, soon to be surprised by the 15-foot Onondaga falls. The cold-water fish must have come from Mountain Spring Lake upstream, owned by the Pennsylvania Game Commission; the closer Lake Jean holds primarily warm-water fish like bass. Beyond Onondaga falls cross the stream, then pass the F. L. Ricketts, Shawnee, Huron, and Ozone waterfalls. The Huron at 41 feet, is (by 1 foot) the tallest of the falls on this side. After Ozone falls cross the stream again on a wooden bridge, pass the R. B. Ricketts waterfall. Recross the stream, go by the B. Reynolds and Wyandot waterfalls, and cross the stream twice more before arriving back at Waters Meet at 5.2 miles.

Turn left here and retrace the 1.75 miles along Kitchen Creek through Ricketts Glen to your car. Good hiking can also be found beyond the Lake Jean campgrounds, across PA 487 in State Game Lands 13, and at the Boston Run Natural Area south of PA 118.

35

Canyon Vista

Total distance: 4 miles
Hiking time: 2 hours
Vertical rise: 1,000 feet
Maps: USGS 7½' Eagles Mere; Loyalsock Trail map;
*   state park map*

This short circuit hike in Worlds End State Park northeast of Williamsport has one severe ascent that can best be called an introduction to the Loyalsock Trail. This is a rugged 58-mile backpacking trail that runs from near Loyalsockville on PA 87 northeast to US 220 just north of Laporte. Well worth the effort in clear weather, the strenuous climb brings you to Canyon Vista overlooking Loyalsock Creek and the mountains beyond. In autumn and spring the view is further heightened by brilliant foliage or flowering pink laurel in June.

To approach Worlds End State Park in Sullivan County from the south, take US 220 northeast 26 miles from Halls. Turn left on PA 154, reaching the park in 8 miles. From Williamsport drive US 220 east about 5 miles to Montoursville, turn left, and drive north 36 miles on PA 87 to Forksville. Turn right on PA 154, winding along trout-filled Loyalsock Creek 2 miles to your parking spot near the park office, a mobile home 1,000 feet from the main picnic entrance to the park.

There are several ways to reach Canyon Vista, including a car ride over 4 miles of dirt roads with switchbacks and very steep grades. Take Mineral Spring Road south from PA 154 for 2 miles to Cold Run

Road, where you turn left and double back north another 2 miles to Canyon Vista and the Labyrinth. If you're not in good physical condition, and aren't used to hand-over-hand climbing with exposed tree roots as handholds, I wouldn't try this hike. On the other hand, if you feel challenged rather than exhausted at the end of this trek, you may want to write for more information and a set of Loyalsock Trail maps: Alpine Outing Club of Williamsport, P.O. Box 278, Williamsport, PA 17701.

Pick up the Loyalsock Trail as it heads south across PA 154 next to the park office, through a picnic area, then uphill. The path is visible the entire way, marked with small, red metal circles tacked to trees, labeled "LT" for Loyalsock Trail. After a strong .2-mile ascent reach trail intersection, following the LT left. The Worlds End Trail, which ends in 2 miles on a road south of the park, continues straight ahead; an unmarked trail runs to the right.

The trail climbs less severely now and flattens out about halfway up to circle around the mountain. Large oaks, pines, and hemlocks—with first branches at several times the height of an average person—tower over thin underbrush of mountain laurel. Birds range the treetops,

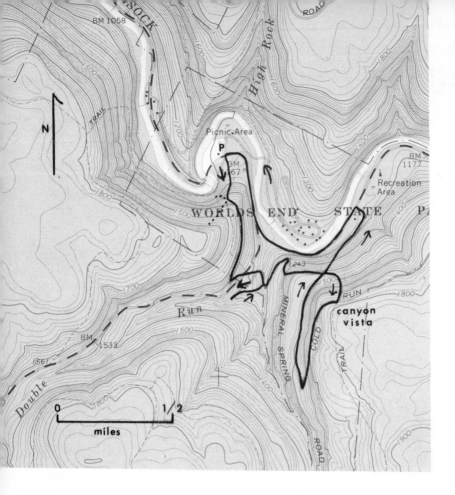

usually out of sight. In about 150 yards on the right you'll see the first of several rock masses on the hike. The mountains in this once glaciated area were formed with little or no folding or faulting. Instead, a raising up of the land pushed up the high plateaus characteristic of the northern tier of Pennsylvania. The sandstone and limestone boulders, originally sediment, were broken off in huge, regular blocks.

This wild area offers protection to many animals not commonly found in other parts of Pennsylvania. In 1978 two novice backpackers hiking the Loyalsock Trail heard and saw a bobcat, the most elusive of Pennsylvania's wildlife. Bears are common visitors to the park's campground where they scavenge for food left by careless campers, bumping garbage cans over to knock off the lids. Campers have learned to leave the lids off to cut down on the noise when these nocturnal bandits make their nightly rounds.

At .7 mile follow the Loyalsock Trail left downhill, encountering larger rocks the lower you go. By Double Run Road at .9 mile, the boulders are as big as box cars, some higher than a several-story building. Nooks and crannies among the huge rectangular rocks provide homes for animals who favor this kind of "devil's playground" for shelter.

Cross the road and head downhill

toward Double Run through large hemlocks. The temperature must be at least ten to fifteen degrees cooler along this narrow stream that cuts between two hills—a pleasant respite in summer but something to remember if you make the trip in winter or fall. Leave the LT for a short distance to follow Double Run upstream (westerly) to Cottonwood Falls. Where the LT crosses Double Run, about 800 feet beyond the road, leave the trail and turn right upstream on an unofficial path, walking on whichever side of the stream is easier. Upstream 1,600 feet is Cottonwood Falls, a narrow cascade 30

feet high surrounded by hemlocks and rocks that provide a good spot to eat lunch or photograph the falls.

To return to the LT, follow the stream back downhill to where the trail crosses. At the intersection turn right (northeast), avoiding the yellow-blazed nature trail that continues straight ahead along the stream to PA 154. At 1.5 miles you reach Mineral Spring Road. Bear right, cross the road, then right again, roughly paralleling the road for about 900 feet. Here, at 1.75 miles, the LT turns sharply left straight uphill for a brief but demanding ascent—a gain of 600 feet in .2 mile.

You can avoid this severe section by turning right at a trail intersection 200 feet after starting uphill—the way you will take down from the top of Canyon Vista. Near the top of this steep sprint on the Loyalsock Trail the path fades somewhat and trees are marked with red ribbons instead of metal circles. There is no margin for error here; you must pull yourself up, foot by foot, by grabbing the roots of trees. If heights make you dizzy, don't attempt the climb, which must be nearly impossible with a full backpack. Near the top you'll be rock scrambling; log steps ease the last 25 feet to the top.

At 2 miles reach Canyon Vista on Cold Run Road, where a log railing keeps you from falling off into space. Below you Loyalsock Creek valley winds through the surrounding Sullivan Highlands, mountains stretching as far as the eye can see. Atop the plateau you could walk long distances without difficult ups and downs. But when you reach a creek, your climb down will be severe, and the mountain rises just as sharply on the other side. This topography is typical of the northern tier of counties, reaching its most severe form in Pennsylvania's Grand Canyon (see Tom Thwaites, *Fifty Hikes in Central Pennsylvania,* Hike 38). There are few places on that rim where you can climb down to the river; here at least it's possible, though difficult.

When you've taken your fill of photos, walk the few yards to Cold Run Road and turn right. A short distance to the left (beyond the outhouses) is the Labyrinth, a spectacular formation of stone blocks interwoven into caves and crannies. Continue on Cold Run Road 100 yards to the Red X Trail, blazed with large, red X's. Turn right, leaving the road; the LT heads left to continue southwest. The Red X Trail doubles back north to return you to your starting point on PA 154, eventually joining the path you would have followed if you had decided to bypass the severe climb on the LT.

At 2.3 miles turn sharply right onto a blue-blazed trail that follows a gently sloping pause in the mountain's climb. You've already accomplished the worst of the descent, which is much more gradual than a return via the Loyalsock Trail. Small seasonal springs dot this section with wet, muddy patches of skunk cabbage and wildflowers. Somewhat to my surprise, I saw a male ring-necked pheasant— usually an inhabitant of fields and woods' edge rather than mountains.

At 2.8 miles reach the LT again—the point where you began the difficult climb. Continue straight ahead on the blue-blazed trail another .3 mile, steadily downhill now. At 3.1 miles the trail ends on Mineral Spring Road. Bear right downhill along the road reaching PA 154 in .1 mile. Cross the road, walk 75 yards to Loyalsock Creek, turn left, and follow the stream back .75 mile to your car. Deep in places, shallow in others, the twisting stream makes a varied obstacle for an experienced angler intent on a trout dinner. On this side hemlocks, and tall rocky cliffs on the opposite shore, make access to the creek difficult in places.

Chilisuagi Trail

Total distance: 4.7 miles
Hiking time: 2 hours
Vertical rise: minimal
Maps: USGS 7½' Washingtonville; preserve map

Fishing, waterfowl observation, and fossil hunting highlight this short walk around Lake Chillisquaque in Montour County northeast of Sunbury. The hiking is not too strenuous even for elementary school children, who delight in the visitor's center where exhibits are designed with them in mind. For part of your walk on Montour Preserve, owned by the Pennsylvania Power and Light Company, the cooling towers of a coal-fired electric plant preside over ancient fossil remains and waterfowl usually associated with remote wilderness.

The area is best approached from east or west by driving I-80 to PA 54 (exit 33), 8 miles west of Bloomsburg. Follow PA 54 north 10 miles to PA 44, turn right, and continue 2 miles northeast to Exchange. Turn right on the only road south out of the village. Follow signs to Montour Preserve for 2 miles, bearing right twice where smaller roads intersect the main one. Turn left at the first four-way crossroads, 1.5 miles south of Exchange; in .5 mile turn left again into the preserve. Drive .3 mile to the end of the road and park at the Goose Cove picnic area, past the visitor's center on the right where trail maps are available, forking left in front of the dam impoundment.

Look for the wooden sign and map of the Chilisuagi Trail at the edge of the field on the north side of the parking lot. The yellow-blazed path circles 165-acre Lake Chillisquaque, developed as an emergency cooling water supply for the nearby power plant. The name comes from Chilisuagi Creek, Iroquois for "Song of the Wild Goose," still appropriate today. The honking of geese is heard continuously along the lakeshore, underscored by calls of mallards, gulls, and loons. Hunting and camping are prohibited year-round, and boating and hiking are restricted during the spring migration in March and April.

Begin hiking north along the narrow two-track through a field. At .2 mile on the right reach the Oak Woods Trail leading to a wildlife observation building on the lake. Use of the trail and building is possible only by a permit obtained at the preserve office next to the visitor's center. Preserve officials strictly limit access to certain areas of the lake conducive to wildlife propagation. At .4 mile a service road, usable only by permit, leads down through White Oak Woods to the observation building.

Beyond the road cross a bridge over a small stream into large tulip poplars and white oaks. Squirrels and chipmunks are everywhere, more angry than afraid of human intruders. The open rolling field on the right is also part of the wildlife refuge; a permit is required to leave the trail. To the right .25 mile are Goose Pasture and the arm of the lake known as Goose Cove. A short pause brought sightings of bluebirds, a common wood thrush, and a grey thrush, with greyer face and less distinct spots on the breast.

In another .2 mile the Chilisuagi Trail parallels a road, then turns right. At .8 mile reach a parking area where the Alder Swamp Trail leads down to Smokehouse Blind at the edge of Goose Pasture—also entered only by permit. Cross the parking lot into another wooded area, up the slight rise of Blue Spruce Hill. From 1 to 1.3 miles the trail follows old fields overgrown with tall grasses, clumps of raspberry bushes, multiflora rose, small cedars, and oak seedlings—a farmland to woodland transition belt.

At 1.4 miles avoid the faint unnamed trail to the left. Pass the remains of an old farmstead at 1.5 miles, in .1 mile entering a woods near the headwaters of the lake. In another .1 mile reach Middle Branch

Chillisquaque Creek, an easy crossing even without a bridge. Across the stream large oaks and tulip poplars rise over the woodland wildflowers covering the stream bottom: here one can find saw-toothed and purple violets, wild pinks, Jack-in-the-pulpits, spring-beauties, and wood-sorrel in mid-May.

Leave the stream bottom for another field where the trail bears right (southwest) through less-endearing poison ivy. At 2 miles enter the tall oaks of Fox Hollow on a trail muddy and rutted by horses' hooves and hikers' boots in spring. Beyond Fox Hollow are two hayfields separated by a narrow strip of trees. To the right is a pine and larch plantation—the trees have been planted, not naturally sown—also part of the wildlife refuge. The larch, or tamarack, is a tall, graceful conifer that loses its soft needle tufts yearly in autumn.

Shagbark hickories fill Hickory Hollow Woods at 2.2 miles. Bend left to a trail intersection at 2.3 miles. To the right is a .8-mile loop down to Ridgefield Point, where waterfowl observation looking west toward Goose Cove is usually excellent. Stay on the Chilisuagi Trail, reaching

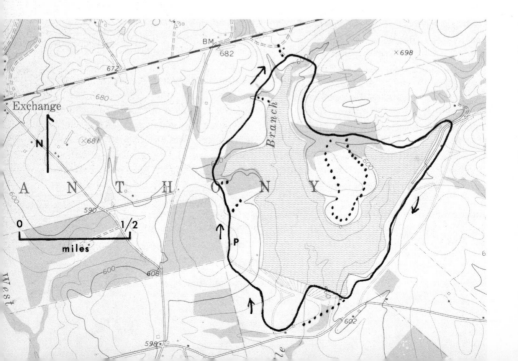

marshy Jellyfish Cove in another .1 mile. You're very close to the edge of Lake Chillisquaque here, breeding grounds for mallards in spring. Canada geese occasionally stay to nest and raise goslings in these quiet inlets, but most of the geese only pause here on their spring and fall migrations, preferring the open water of the main body of the lake. Killdeer and small sandpipers stalk the sandy flats, poking among the rocks and sand for small insects.

At 3 miles cross another small stream and turn sharply right, leaving woods, overgrown fields, and swampy inlets to walk along the lakeshore. After the right turn and stream crossing, walk another 100 yards, enough to get out of the tangle onto a grassy slope. To leave the trail for the fossil pits, turn left (due south) here, reaching a paved road in about 400 feet. Turn right and continue to the parking area for the fossil pit on your left. This worthwhile side trip should at least produce shale fragments with fossil prints of small shells, ferns, and what look like worm holes. Persistent amateur paleontologists have here found the signatures of small prehistoric marine animals such as the crablike trilobite. Collecting is permitted and most of the shale is so loose that the only gear you'll need is a collecting bag.

Head north out of the parking area through an old field to return to the Chilisuagi Trail, or leave the trail to follow the lakeshore for better views of waterfowl on the lake. As I headed southwest, I heard the eerie call of a loon—somehow incongruous so near the cooling towers of the nearby electric power plant. The large, black and white bird was feeding in the middle of the inlet, diving for fish every few seconds, only to reappear flapping its wings 25 to 30 feet beyond. Loons need plenty of take-off space to gain the air, rarely venturing onto land since they can barely walk. Flocks of herring gulls frequent the flat, windswept shoreline of Heron Cove, and loons and sandpipers, although numerous here, are actually uncommon to this area.

At 3.8 miles pass the Heron Cove picnic and boat access areas. Just beyond to the left is Sunset Point overlook. At 4 miles reach the lake impoundment. To get to the visitor's center you can continue southwest on the trail, or turn right across the dam for good views of the entire lake. Halfway across turn left at a discharge pipe to walk down the impoundment toward the barnlike visitor's center visible from the dam. Return to your car by turning right on the road back to the Goose Cove parking lot, or shorten the .4-mile walk by cutting through the fields, avoiding the winding road.

37

Blue Hill

Total distance: 1.6 miles
Hiking time: 1¾ hours
Vertical rise: 300 feet
Maps: USGS 7½' Northumberland; state park map

This short hike near Northumberland and Sunbury circles an active woodland area nestled in the cliffs overlooking the confluence of the West and North branches of the Susquehanna. Take your time here—don't hike straight through as though you still have another 10 miles to cover before dark. You'll see an interesting variety of plants and wildlife, and impressive views of the Susquehanna, the river towns of Northumberland and Sunbury, and the woods and farmland beyond. This would be a good hike for families; you might even let older children explore by themselves while you picnic.

To reach the area in Shikellamy State Park on the west bank of the Susquehanna, take US 11—US 15 north from Harrisburg (or from I-81), along the west side of the river. Where US 15 and US 11 split, continue north on US 11. About .4 mile south of where US 11 heads east across the Susquehanna, turn left onto County Line Road and immediately under a railroad underpass. From the north or the south, this turnoff on a broad curve is nearly blind, but small signs on US 11 point to Shikellamy State Park. In .4 mile turn right onto the well-marked park road. Head sharply uphill, making a 1-mile

circle to the left. Park on the south side of the loop near a picnic shelter. From the east, head west on I-80 to PA 54 (exit 33), 8 miles west of Bloomsburg. Turn south to reach US 11 in 3 miles. At US 11 turn right and continue southwest, reaching County Line Road in 12 miles—.4 mile after you cross the Susquehanna River.

Begin walking southwest downhill on the Oak Ridge Trail at the rear of the picnic shelter. White oaks, tall and stately, tower over laurel and blueberry bushes. Squirrels and chipmunks are nearly as thick here as fallen oak leaves. They are everywhere—running ahead, darting off to the side, scolding from the safety of the tallest tree. Although the trail isn't blazed, the path cut is well maintained and easy to follow as it winds through a thriving forest.

At .3 mile the Oak Ridge Trail ends on the Deer Trail. Turn right here and begin to circle the perimeter of the park. The Deer Trail heads uphill almost immediately to the west and then north, dipping at one point into a narrow hollow to cross a stream. Along the Deer Trail the trees are even larger—and the area wilder—than along the Oak Ridge Trail. Underbrush grows thickly, and large hemlocks abound.

You soon cross a bridge over another

seasonal stream. The stream bed is rocky—hardly more than a wash—but tracks of deer and raccoon line its muddy banks. In early spring edible bracken ferns push above ground and unfurl, surrounding the bank of the little run.

At .6 mile, on the right, pass the Dry Hollow Trail and walk back to the parking lot. Beyond, begin a gradual ascent into a cool and attractive stand of pines—good cover for deer. I almost bumped into two before they spotted me and took off. Honeysuckle climbs profusely along an outcropping of rocks on the right, intermixed with multiflora rose. At .7 mile the trail angles left—near the edge of an old field—and soon heads right again, out to the edge of Blue Hill. The cliffs overlook

the Susquehanna River at the confluence of the West and North branches, dropping nearly 400 feet straight down to the river. You cling to the very edge of the mountain here, protected by a chain-link fence.

The view from Blue Hill is stunning and far-reaching. Across the river, extending northeast up the North Branch, is Packers Island. The southwest tip of the island is also part of Shikellamy State Park, primarily used for boat launching and picnicking. The Basse A. Beck Environmental Education Center there teaches visitors about the river, its influences on people, and other environmental concerns. West of Packers Island is Northumberland, centered on the point of land between the two rivers, and further west, farmland and woodlands. South of Packers Island is the town of Sunbury.

Small laurel bushes and other low shrubs cover the cliffs between the trail and the river, making excellent hiding places for small warblers and other birds. At one point, the trail heads off the top of the cliffs so that you are cliff-side, among the birds. Here, I saw male and female rufous-sided towhees—birds that somewhat resemble orioles with black, orange, and white markings—and many small sparrows. Several red-tailed hawks soared high over the river, at eye-level.

Pass the overlook and head downhill slightly. At 1.1 miles the trail turns right, away from the cliffs, and reenters the woods. Views are still possible in places but they are not as panoramic as higher up Blue Hill. Turn right again and cross the entrance road at 1.2 miles. In .2 mile turn right, uphill, on the Oak Ridge Trail and retrace your path to the picnic pavilion and car. The park was nearly deserted in spring, but in summer, picnickers will probably lessen your chances of seeing wildlife unless you visit on a weekday.

38

Locust Lake

Total distance: 2.8 miles
Hiking time: 1¾ hours
Vertical rise: 300 feet
Maps: USGS 7½' Shenandoah, USGS 7½' Delano;
  state park map

Even during a driving, cold spring rain, this short loop in Locust Lake State Park, 13 miles southwest of Hazelton, was an enjoyable walk. The hike circles the camping areas near the lake—boasting cold-water brook trout—then follows Locust Creek upstream through a pretty glen of magnificent oaks and hemlocks, returning via a power-line cut and a short cross-country trek across the mountains. In good weather, children will enjoy the easy stride and the lively, colorful inhabitants of the lake and creek.

Locust Lake is in Schuylkill County just south of I-81; take exit 37 west on PA 54 toward Mahanoy City. Turn left immediately, past a gas station on your right. In 1 mile turn left again, following signs to Locust Lake State Park. Continue on Legislative Route 53087, crossing under I-81 in .5 mile. Drive another .5 mile and turn left at the first intersection, passing the Mountain Valley Golf Course. In 1.3 miles bear right at an intersection just before Walborn School, and right again in .1 mile to enter the park. Continue 1.2 miles, turning left across the lake on the impoundment. At the south shore turn right into a fisherman's parking area. From Reading, take PA 61 north 37 miles to Frackville. Here, head north 7 miles on

I-81 to exit 37, then follow the rest of the driving instructions.

From your parking spot walk west along a paved bicycle trail that circles the lake. The lake, created by the impoundment of Locust Creek, sits in a deep valley between oak- and hemlock-covered mountains. West of the dam the lake begins to lose its man-made look. At the western edge large hemlocks and boulders jut into the lake on small points of land, popular spots for shore fishermen angling for brown and brook trout in the cold water.

On the right pass a log amphitheater where the park naturalist gives summer lectures. Shortly beyond is a good view of the man-made swamp on the left. Locust Creek rushes off the mountain in a narrow cut, but widens at the western lakeshore, killing trees in the flood. Downy woodpeckers frequent the stands of drowned tree skeletons and grasses, and raccoon footprints line the muddy edge of the bike path.

At .4 mile cross a small bridge on the bicycle path, then look for an unmarked trail on the left, along the bank of Locust Creek. Trout darted in front of me in the fast-moving, stone-strewn brook, apparently traveling southwest upstream from the main lake. In early spring, the regenerating forest floor presented the beginnings of mayapples and Jack-in-the-pulpits pushing through the peaty, rotting bed of last year's leaves. The most prevalent plant—one of the earliest to peek through—is the skunk cabbage, known for its offensive odor. The first ferns were just starting to unwind, a tender delicacy for forest foragers.

At .6 mile come to a bridge across the stream and the beginning of a white-blazed trail. As you continue upstream, hike on whichever side of the creek seems best. The blazed trail and the unmarked path on the other side are virtually interchangeable; the blazed trail crosses and recrosses the creek several times, the white blazes disappearing only to reappear again several hundred feet

upstream. There is little danger of getting lost: roads of some kind, paved or dirt, surround the area. This hike makes a smaller loop within the circle of roads, and while sections look like remote wilderness, you're never more than 1 to 2 miles from a road back to civilization.

Locust Creek is a playground for children of all ages. Besides trout, I found good-sized crayfish and several kinds of salamander, including the large red-spotted newt. These make food for raccoons, and large trout eat some of the smaller varieties. Children are fascinated by these brightly colored amphibians because they're pretty, and unlike crayfish, are harmless. Crayfish use their pincers at the slightest provocation, a challenge many find hard to resist. If you're fishing or camping here, older

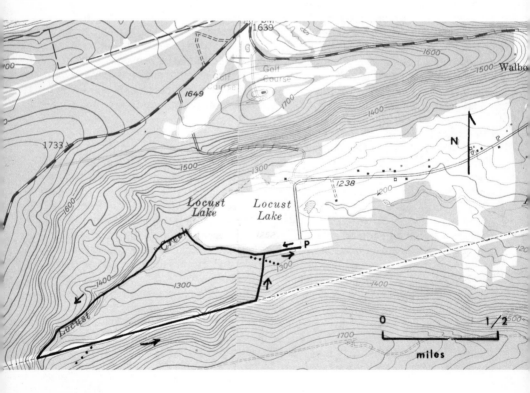

children could be allowed to explore the stream alone, following the streambank back to the camping area.

After 1 mile the stream narrows as it approaches the source. Here, you can also hear the sounds of the road only .25 mile west. When the bank gets so tangled that it is difficult to follow, leave the stream and head south uphill. Turn left when you reach a power line that cuts northeast-southwest through the area, crossing Locust Creek. Follow the cut northeast back toward the lake, passing a dirt road on the right at 1.3 miles. Climb, then descend, the narrow hollows along the cut, through tall, mature oaks—and pines in depressions where the soil is wetter. I didn't expect to see wildlife during a soaking rain, but near a stand of beeches I frightened a very wet deer and a grouse. A small hawk, protected somewhat by pine boughs, left his haven when he spotted me.

Walk .5 mile beyond the dirt road along the side of the mountain; to the left (north) downhill is Locust Lake. Listen for lake sounds—an occasional car, the noise of a child in the campground—to determine where to head north. Anywhere after .2 mile beyond the dirt road intersecting the power-line cut, you can turn north and be within easy access of the lake and your car. The descent is not terribly steep, but wet leaves can make it slippery.

Near the bottom at 2.2 miles, the mountainside is likely to be slightly boggy—sprouting skunk cabbage suggested that the wetness is permanent. Head through the narrow area if you don't mind a damp foot, but if you can't pick your way through without getting wet, head westerly about .2 mile, turn north again, and reach the campground road in another .2 mile. From the road, walk straight ahead to the edge of the lake, turn right, and follow the bike trail east .3 mile back to your car.

Boulder Field

Total distance: 4.75 miles
Hiking time: 3 hours
Vertical rise: 150 feet
Maps: USGS 7½' Hickory Run; state park map

Boulder Field, the highlight of this hike at Hickory Run State Park in the Poconos, is one of the most unusual geologic features in eastern Pennsylvania. A relic from the Wisconsin ice sheet, the nearly flat field of boulders, 400 feet wide and over .25 mile long, is virtually unchanged after 20,000 years. Barren of vegetation, Boulder Field is an anomaly in the middle of the forest, appearing suddenly in the dense pines.

The hike requires two cars, one at the trailhead near the campground and entrance to the park on PA 534, and a second car at the end of the hike on the north edge of Boulder Field. If you can't spot a second car, you'll have to return via the same route, or walk down a lightly used gravel road to PA 534 and back to your car.

To reach Hickory Run State Park in Carbon County take exit 41 off I-80 and drive south on PA 534 for 6 miles. If you are approaching from the Northeast Extension of the Pennsylvania Turnpike (PA 9), take exit 35, drive 3 miles west on PA 940, then turn south on PA 534 and continue 6 miles. On PA 534 pass the park office on the right, Sand Spring Road on the left (to Sand Spring Day Use swimming area), then the entrance to a family camping area on the right. Beyond the campground entrance .25 mile, turn left on a dirt road and drive 700 feet to a picnic area, parking lot, and the trailhead.

You should spot the second car at Boulder Field; watch for signs on PA 534 directing you to the area. Turn left off PA 534 on the Sand Spring Day Use Area Road, just before reaching the campground. After 1.5 miles the paved road narrows and turns to dirt, continuing 2.5 more miles to Boulder Field.

If you walk from the family camping area to the trailhead, add .7 mile to your total mileage for the hike. Begin walking east on the Gamewire Trail, which begins on the right side of the parking lot at the edge of a field of picnic tables. Orange blazes appear first on posts, then high on trees so that they aren't at knee level or obscured altogether in the deep snow of winter, when the flat, relatively rock-free Gamewire Trail is used by snowmobilers.

In .25 mile enter a woods, leaving the picnic area behind. Bracken ferns blanket the forest floor between thinly spaced small oaks, maples, and hemlocks. Before the Civil War this area was called "Shades of Death" because of the dense, extensive cover of virgin white pine and hemlock. After 1865 many logging camps sprang up to scour the timber, and nearly every stream in the area was dammed to supply power for a local sawmill. The remains of several dams on Hickory Run and Sand Spring Run can be seen today in the park.

At .9 mile the Gamewire Trail heads north in a gentle swing to the left, ending at 1.75 miles on a wide gravel road. Turn right, crossing under the Northeast Extension of the Pennsylvania Turnpike viaduct. Just beyond, join the Stage Trail on the right. Long vistas on this heavily forested path are limited by dense hemlocks and lack of elevation. The Stage Trail is all that remains of an old stage road that ran 70 miles between Bethlehem and Wilkes-Barre. The inn at Saylorsville, a nearby lumber town, could accommodate 150 guests who came through on the stage route. The only remnant of that community today is the old dam on Hickory Run.

At 2.8 miles leave the Stage Trail to join the Boulder Field Trail north (left); the segment to the right heads south toward Hawk Falls. In the deep pines and undergrowth of laurel and blueberry bushes, I saw a pair of rufous-sided towhees, a scarlet tanager, and an indigo bunting—a tiny, iridescent royal blue bird that prefers deep woods, rarely venturing into old fields and other more inhabited places.

Reach Boulder Field at 4.5 miles, 1.7 miles after joining the Boulder Field Trail. I watched for indications I was nearing the field, but the slightly rocky path is typical of Pennsylvania hiking trails and doesn't begin to prepare you for Boulder Field itself. Suddenly the woods end, and great boulders stretch out before you in a barren plain .25 mile long and wider than a football field is long. Average boulders are about 4 feet square, the largest are 25 feet long. No soil fills the spaces between rocks and nothing grows here, not even lichen. Some of the rocks in the nearly flat

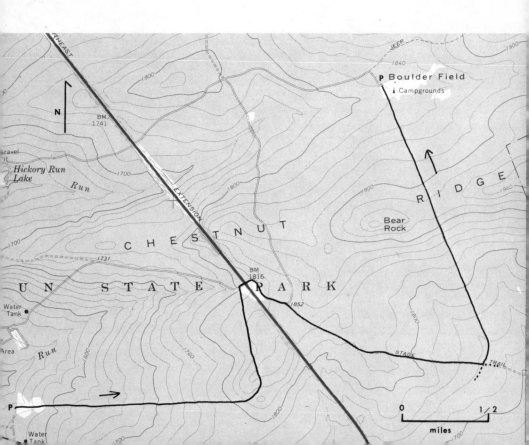

field are small enough to pick up. In places, curious observers have moved some of them in an effort to find the bottom of the field—a fool's project since the rocks are 12 feet deep in places. In certain seasons, water rushes audibly below you in an underground river.

At the east end of the field the rocks are square, sharp-edged blocks, but at the west and south ends, they are weathered and pock-marked. According to park geologists, glacial action constantly ground the rocks in the western section against each other when parts of the ice mass melted each summer. The rocks in the eastern section did not receive this glacial action and were not as severely weathered, retaining their original blocklike shape. The boulders in the northern end are predominantly red sandstone, but at the south end there are more red conglomerate and white quartz pebbles mixed in. Trees and soil have encroached on the field gradually, reducing its size. Similar fields of rocks elsewhere in eastern Pennsylvania are the River of Rocks on Hawk Mountain (see Hike 14) and Blue Rocks near the Pinnacle (Hike 13). The fields were

formed when blocks were tumbled gradually downhill by the erosion of softer rock underneath these large rocks.

Walking through Boulder Field is difficult; there is sometimes as much as 4 feet relief from one boulder to the next. It is much faster and safer to skirt the edge and make forays into the field along the way. As you near the parking lot at the north end of the field, you'll find graffiti spray-painted by those who find an area unchanged in 20,000 years a temptation for vandalism.

At 4.75 miles reach the end of Boulder Field and the car you spotted earlier. Parts of the lightly traveled gravel road are one-way, but the exit road is clearly marked and returns you to PA 534. Access to the road in winter is probably limited to snowmobiles. If you are walking back to the campground, follow the road back to Sand Spring Lake and day use area. Here leave the road and follow Sand Spring Run to PA 534. Turn left on PA 534 and walk .25 mile to the campground. If you walk back to the campground or to the car parked by the picnic area, your total mileage will be doubled.

Devils Hole

Total distance: 2.6 miles
Hiking time: 1¼ hours
Vertical rise: 230 feet
Map: USGS 7½' Buck Hill Falls

You could prolong this pleasant walk along a deep, serpentine gorge by lingering to enjoy the sights and sounds: a fast-moving, rock-strewn creek; waterfalls cascading over boulders; stately hemlocks; a variety of woodland and freshwater animals. This hike near the town of Mount Pocono on State Game Lands 221 follows Devils Hole Creek upstream, passing the ruins of an old building—purported to be an elegant speakeasy in the 1920s—to return on the opposite bank.

To reach Devils Hole, take I-80 to the intersection with I-380, between exits 43 and 44. Follow I-380 north 4 miles to PA 940 and turn right (east). (If you approach on I-380 south from Scranton, turn east here also.) About 2 miles east of Mount Pocono, 7 miles after leaving I-380, you come to narrow Devils Hole Road on the left. Turn left (north) and drive 1.2 miles to where the road makes a 90-degree right turn, and a sign designates this State Game Lands 221. Park straight ahead off the curve.

From Promised Land State Park (see Hike 43, 44, and 45), follow PA 390 south 15 miles to just beyond Mountainhome, where you continue south on PA 191. At Paradise Valley, 6 miles after you pick up PA 191, turn right (west) onto PA 940. Devils Hole Road, a short loop with two entrances on PA 940, will be on your right in 3 miles. Turn right and drive 1.8 miles. Beyond a railroad crossing at .2 mile, the road bends sharply left. Park on the right, just off the turn.

Begin walking northeast downhill on a woods road barred to traffic by a gate. Reach Devils Hole Creek in 300 yards and turn left upstream. Fishermen who come to hunt for trout among fallen logs and boulders make their own trails on both sides of the creek here. Follow whatever path seems clearest to you; try to stay west upstream and east on your return, but switch sides if the going gets rough. In spring when the creek is full this stream hopping may be difficult, but finding your way through the tangle of boulders, laurel, and blueberries along the narrow streambank is half the challenge. The forest is largely hemlock, with a few beeches and maples so tall that you can't see the leaves at the top.

Devils Hole Creek is a fast-moving, serpentine stream that changes constantly as it rushes through the gorge—narrow and deep around one bend, wider around the next. In some places, boulders are large; in others, the sandstones are small enough to fit in the palm of your hand, weathered and rounded by water into smooth shapes pleasing to the touch. Small waterfalls cascade down boulders, drowning out most other woods sounds. Rising 600 feet above you on either side, the steep ridges block long views but give you the sense that you are hiking deeper and deeper into the gorge. Look for Devils Hole at a wide right-hand bend to the northeast, .75 miles from the trailhead. The origin of the name is lost to local tradition, but here where the narrow gorge is deepest, from the top it

must look like a drain into the devil's world.

Just beyond Devils Hole on the west bank are the ruins of what looks like a brick backyard barbeque. Here, a narrow trail to the right leads past several spruce to the streambank and the ruins of a large building. Local fishermen claim that during Prohibition the building was a speakeasy that made the best illegal liquor anywhere. The establishment used the stream for liquor production and depended upon the remoteness of the area to avoid detection. Near the

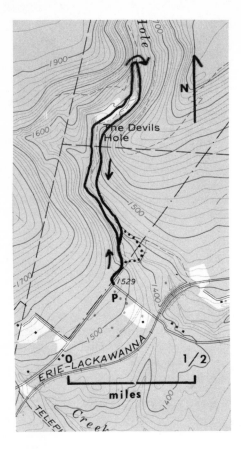

Continue upstream .25 mile beyond the ruins. It is possible to go further, but the stream narrows and is not as spectacular. Cross to the other side where walking is more difficult. On the west side a 50-foot stream bottom separates the steep hill from the creek; the east bank offers much less walking room. Several channels of the stream are visible here, forming small islands, runs, and waterfalls. Some of the grass- and fern-covered islands support mature trees thirty to fifty years old. I also saw evidence of camping, not permitted on Pennsylvania's game lands.

On the east bank a strong windstorm had recently twisted off tree trunks 15 feet above the ground, leaving upright stumps. Other trees had fallen over, pulling up big mounds of earth with the roots. Water collecting in the root holes became home for a variety of freshwater animals: tadpoles, frogs, skippers, and crayfish. These pockets of water unconnected to the main stream frequently become death traps; raccoons can easily snare a meal from these water holes, from which there is no escape. I followed the tracks of four raccoons, probably a sow and her young, which led to a half dozen of these tree-hole pools, one after the other.

Since there is no marked trail through the gorge, keep an eye out for the woods road on your right that will return you to your car. The road is visible when you are at the spot, but you won't see it ahead of you. When you reach the woods road, cross the stream and head back uphill to your car. If you become so entranced with the scenery that you miss the woods road, you'll reach a bridge .1 mile beyond the road. You can cross on the bridge and follow another woods road uphill, where it joins the road you came in on, back to your car.

"barbeque" are the remains of what looks like a pulley system running to the top of the hill. I was told variously that it was once a ski lift (improbable given the steepness of the hill), a gondola for carrying people down to the speakeasy, and the method of removing liquor from the site when a raid threatened. In this deep, wooded gorge on a secluded stream, it's easy to imagine scenes of an elegant but illicit nature taking place here in the 1920s.

41

Tobyhanna Creek and Bender Swamp

Total distance: 3.8 miles
Hiking time: 1½ hours
Vertical rise: 140 feet
Maps: USGS 7½' Tobyhanna; state park map

Atop the never-ending steep mountains of the eastern Pennsylvania Poconos are plateaus and swamps, thickly wooded with northern hardwoods and densely populated with wildlife, including black bear. This hike in Tobyhanna State Park southeast of Scranton takes you north upstream on Tobyhanna Creek, through Bender Swamp on an old meadow path, and returns via a power-line cut and a short bushwhack easy enough for novices. In 1949 the park was created from land acquired from federally controlled Tobyhanna Military Reservation, which continues today as nearby Tobyhanna Army Depot. The federal property served variously as an ambulance corps training center in World War I, housing for Civilian Conservation Corps workers in the Depression, and a German prisoner-of-war camp during World War II.

To reach Tobyhanna State Park (southwest of Promised Land State Park, see Hikes 43, 44, and 45), take I-80 to I-380, between exits 43 and 44. Drive north 10 miles on I-380 to PA 423, turn right, and continue 1 mile northeast to Tobyhanna. Stay on PA 423 another 3 miles to reach the park office and camping area entrance at the north end of Tobyhanna Lake. Turn left (north) on the entrance road, driving .7 mile to a bridge across Tobyhanna Creek where it flows into Tobyhanna Lake. Pull off the road and park on the right just beyond the stream. If you are driving from Scranton take I-380 south 22 miles to the intersection of PA 423. Turn northeast and follow the directions to the parking area.

Find the trailhead across Tobyhanna Creek on the west side just beyond the bridge. The trail is wide and flat, covered with wood chips where it's likely to be muddy—in dry weather, the unpaved trail out to the power-line cut is suitable for bicycling. Follow the edge of Tobyhanna Creek north a few steps, then west. The wide, swampy creek meanders slowly, with grass growing through the water and few areas where the banks are well defined. In .1 mile leave the open, swampy creek for a dry maple and beech woods teeming with red and grey squirrels, chipmunks, thrushes, chickadees, and sparrows. You may cross some soggy ground in Bender Swamp, but for most of the hike you're protected from the wetlands.

Around a right turn you'll suddenly find yourself on the edge of Bender Swamp. The trail crosses only part of the narrow swamp created by broad, flat Tobyhanna

Creek and Jim Smith Run. In dry seasons, except where the stream flows into the lake, only the marshy area and a nearly dry channel show where the stream courses. Tall grass and raspberry bushes cover the swamp to a height of 4 to 5 feet. At .5 mile raccoon tracks were everywhere, circling muddy spots where receding water trapped minnows and tadpoles.

At .6 mile, before the trail crosses Tobyhanna Creek by a wooden bridge, a faint trail heads right (east) at the edge of the swamp. On your left are skeletons of drowned trees, on the right, lush forest. Turn right on the trail for .25 mile along the edge of the swamp through what looks like an old meadow. Low walls of rounded stones, tossed in heaps along the edge of

the field, still run in straight lines. The path makes a comfortable foray along the edge of the swamp—you're close enough to see well, without the pitfalls of muddy feet or attacking mosquitoes.

Dead water-swamped trees provide work and food for woodpeckers who leave nesting holes for a wide variety of other birds. I saw an indigo bunting, and a red-tailed hawk scouting from the top of a tree skeleton. The largest hawk you will commonly see in eastern Pennsylvania, the adult red-tailed hawk can be 1.5 to 2 feet tall with a 4-foot wingspread. Even so, a group of three or four sparrows, chickadees, or other small birds can gang up on a hawk in flight, maintaining the assault until the hawk leaves the area. Follow the side trail .25 mile to where it

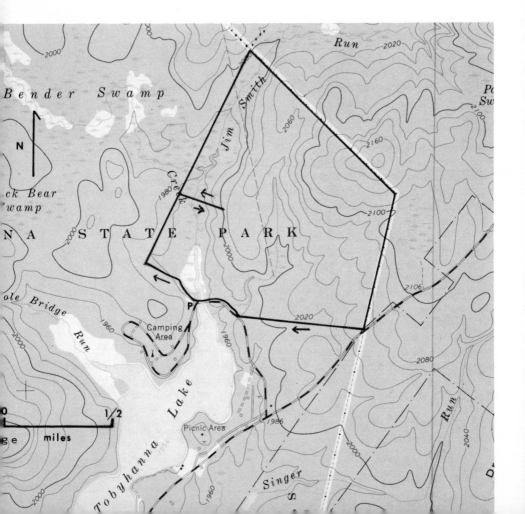

leaves the edge of the swamp to enter woods again, then retrace your steps to the main trail at 1.1 miles, turning right.

At 1.3 miles you begin to walk out of Bender Swamp, slightly uphill. Jim Smith Run is on your right, but the stream and swamp are hidden most of the time. At 1.9 miles reach a power transmission line cut, turn right (southeast), and follow the cut back toward PA 423. (Your original trail continues straight ahead, reaching PA 196 in 1.5 miles.) After the right turn, the cut crosses another swampy stream, a branch of Jim Smith Run. In the open cut I saw a pair of swamp sparrows, with red or

rusty head and rusty sides, grey face, and grey eye stripe. This sparrow prefers open swamps and bogs, probably attracted here by the openness provided by the power-line cut.

At 2.2 miles you leave most of the swamp behind, except an occasional boggy patch. Deer tracks are plentiful along the wood-lined cut, and bear are also fairly common. Black Bear Swamp—adjacent to Bender Swamp— didn't get its name without reason. Another couple hiking earlier in the day saw a small black bear here cross the cut ahead of them to the southeast, turning over rocks and logs in search of food.

Bears usually give hikers no cause for alarm, but black bears with cubs can be dangerous, attacking without warning. Do not walk between a cub and its mother. A cub without its mother is not lost—assume the mother is close by. If you can spot the mother, head off in the opposite direction if possible. If you don't see her, stay in the open where you have a good view of the forest and when you see her coming, head back out along the path that retraces your steps. Hikers sometimes carry "bear bells" on their packs, small bells that let bears know someone is in their territory, since they hate to be surprised.

At 2.8 miles follow the power-line cut as it swings right, slightly west of south, then past another small swamp to the east. At 3.3 miles reach PA 423. The power-line cut continues across the road into State Game Lands 127 (see Hike 42), but you need to return to the bridge on Tobyhanna

Creek and your car. You could bear right on PA 423 and walk .5 mile south to the park office, then right again, continuing north .7 mile to the bridge.

A more interesting return is to make a ninety-degree turn to the right (west northwest) where the power-line cut intersects PA 423, angling back into the woods for a short, .7-mile bushwhack. First-timers should use a compass, but any direction except north (which leads back into the swamp) will return you to a road—PA 423 or the park entrance road. The underbrush is thick but not too difficult, and the grade slightly downhill with few distinguishing landmarks. As long as you head west or slightly north of west, you'll reach the road, where you turn right and walk a short distance to your car. If you reach Tobyhanna Creek before you reach the road, turn left downstream until the creek crosses the road at the bridge where you parked.

Huckleberry Marsh

Total distance: 3.2 miles
Hiking time: 2 hours
Vertical rise: 40 feet
Map: USGS 7½' Tobyhanna

If you hate to get your feet wet, you may miss some of the special features of this hike around Huckleberry Marsh in State Game Lands 127, south of Tobyhanna State Park. Although the Poconos of eastern Pennsylvania boast many swamps, the most exciting are cold, spring-fed sphagnum bogs where you'll see a variety of plants not often found south of Canada. Spring (or early summer) is the best season to hike here; the vegetation is impassable later and fall fills the game lands with hunters.

Although most of the trail is dry, you may find wet areas near Pond Swamp and Huckleberry Marsh. You could bring an extra pair of sneakers to prevent soggy boots, but I got wet feet only when I ventured off the trail to see a particularly unusual plant. Bring a field guide to wildflowers to identify the interesting species in this dense and remote area. The 3-mile loop is not difficult because of length or grade, but requires careful hiking to avoid wet areas and fallen trees. I would not hike alone here, and I advise bringing the United States Geological Survey (USGS) map for the area, because many trails crisscross the game lands.

To reach Huckleberry Marsh take I-380 southeast from Scranton for 22 miles.

Here, join PA 423 and drive south .4 mile. When you reach a sign to the game lands, turn right on the dirt road, and continue 3.6 miles. From the south, take the Northeast Extension of the Pennsylvania Turnpike to exit 35 where you join I-80 east for 17 miles; then turn north onto I-380. Drive 7 miles to the turnoff on PA 423. From Harrisburg take I-81 to I-80, reaching I-380 in 31 miles.

Many trails crisscross the game lands road before you reach the trailhead. The USGS map helps to eliminate the problem of finding the right trail, but many other equally interesting trails could also show you the bog vegetation of this hike. After 2.6 miles on the dirt road, cross a run and head uphill slightly to an area where you're not surrounded by dry land. At 3.4 miles, head downhill; both sides of the road are swampy here. Just past a left bend, a faint two-track heads off to the left, southwest. Pull off and park by the road. (In another .1 mile, another trail to the left heads west-northwest.)

Start hiking on the old road through Pond Swamp. After .2 mile of mostly dry and easy walking—through maples, swamp grass, and pines—the trail splits. Take the right fork; the trail to the left will be your return route. By .3 mile you have

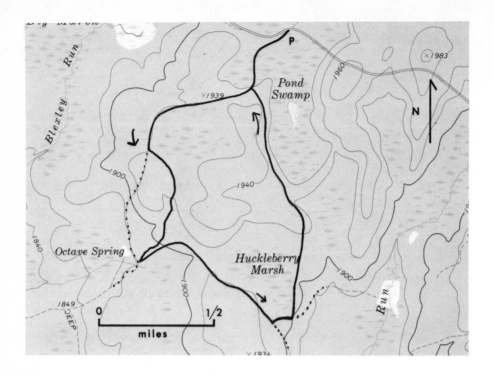

climbed out of the swamp. Beyond, the trail bends to the right (west) through swamp maples and oaks.

At .8 mile the trail splits again. Take the left fork, although they rejoin in .4 mile. Wherever the land is dry, tall maples and beeches reach above the forest floor. In the wetter sections, the few trees standing have long since become skeletons—havens for woodpeckers and other birds.

At 1.2 miles reach a trail intersection and Octave Spring where I saw a pitcher-plant, 1 foot tall with a single pitcher—a hollow tube formed by part of the leaf. The plant is a carnivore, trapping hapless insects that fall into the pitcher. In May the reddish buds were just ready to bloom. These unusual plants are restricted to swamps, usually in more northern climates. Although never common, the plant is well established in the Poconos.

Nearby I found Labrador-tea, a plant that also prefers cold northern bogs. A cluster of five-petaled pinkish flowers tops the small thin-leaved plant. In the area of Octave Spring, the swamp rose is the most numerous plant. This rose, with pale pink flowers beginning in June, also prefers wet feet. A variety of pink orchid, calopogon, also grows here, but more commonly seen is another member of the orchid family, the moccasin-flower or pink lady's-slipper, which blooms in May and June.

At the trail intersection turn hard left. (If you took the right-hand split at .8 mile you'll have two trails to the left. Avoid the one nearest you, which returns north, and take the left next to it.) Just past the trail junction I saw a pileated woodpecker, a black and white, crow-sized bird with a large red head and topcrest—probably the prototype for the cartoon character

Woody Woodpecker. They often travel in pairs and usually prefer deep forest. The nearly identical ivory-billed woodpecker is an endangered species on the verge of extinction.

At 1.4 miles, the trail curves southeast uphill slightly into a drier oak and maple forest. At 2 miles reach aptly named Huckleberry Marsh, where sunlight penetrates the marsh to produce ripe berries in July. Wild blueberries and huckleberries are similar—the flavor is identical, but huckleberries have a single seed in the fruit and a more blue-black color. Blueberries are bluer with many tiny seeds. In many areas, *huckleberry* means any blueberry growing uncultivated. Huckleberry Marsh is also the kind of habitat a bobcat might appreciate —nearby at Bruce Lake Natural Area (see Hike 43) bobcat tracks are occasionally seen. Deer and black bear are large animals common to this area.

At 2.1 miles, at the south end of the loop, the trail forks again. Take the left fork and in .1 mile turn left at another fork. Head north across the eastern edge of Huckleberry Marsh. For .2 mile the trail may be slightly wet, but you soon head uphill slightly past Huckleberry Marsh to follow the southern end of Pond Swamp. At 3 miles bear right to rejoin the trail across boggy Pond Swamp. In .2 mile reach the dirt road and your car.

Bruce Lake Natural Area

Total distance: 8.3 miles
Hiking time: 4 hours
Vertical rise: 200 feet
Maps: USGS 7 ½' Promised Land; state park map

An early morning walk around Balsam Swamp in Bruce Lake Natural Area near Promised Land State Park in Pike County brought glimpses of uncommon wildlife—brightly-colored warblers, tiny tree and land frogs, a grey fox, a ring-necked duck. I must have seen 100 birds and animals in this remote lush swamp and woodland in the Poconos. Bruce Lake is designated a state forest natural area in Pennsylvania: no vehicles are permitted within its 2,700 acres, and tent camping only, limited to 48 hours, can be arranged by permit from the park office.

To reach the trailhead, take exit 7 off I-84, 26 miles east of Scranton, and head south on PA 390, passing the Egypt Meadow Road entrance in .25 mile. At 1.5 miles reach the Bruce Lake Road entrance on the left and park in a pulloff left of PA 390. From the south, take I-80 east and then I-380 north. Turn right (east) on PA 940, continue 4 miles to Paradise Valley, then north on PA 191 for 4 miles. In Mountainhome turn right onto PA 390, continuing north 18 miles through the town of Promised Land to the pulloff on the right at Bruce Lake Road.

Begin hiking east on Bruce Lake Road, a dirt woods road closed to vehicles. You could hike this 8-mile circuit of flat terrain quickly, but it is more rewarding to travel slowly and carefully, to observe the abundant life in the swamps and dense woods of beech, birch, maple, and hemlock. Panther Swamp is to the left, visible almost from your first step.

If you leave the trail for a closer view, at the edge of the swamp is a scene of pre-history come to life. Tall skeletons of deciduous trees and pines stand rotting in the water. Decaying fallen logs, swamp grass, and dark water stained by tannic acid dominate the landscape. Birds chatter incessantly. I could barely take a step without frightening something—a group of surprised mallards, moulting and unable to fly, struggled noisily away. Mosquitoes attacked joyfully, ignoring my repellent.

Hemlocks and balsams skirt the edge and penetrate the swamp, preventing open views. Keep walking until you reach the eastern edge where a side trail heads north, far enough away to breed fewer mosquitoes. Follow it for a few hundred yards for a good view of the swamp and its activities.

At .5 mile the Brown Trail joins Bruce Lake Road on the right, your return route after circling Balsam Swamp. Continue on the woods road through tall maples and beeches with little underbrush. At .9 mile Panther Swamp Trail heads left, reaching the north end of Egypt Meadow Lake in .5 mile. Stay on Bruce Lake Road where you begin to notice Balsam Swamp on your right at 1 mile. Balsam Swamp is larger but less dramatic than Panther Swamp. You'll see small sinks of water amid hummocks of what look like dry land, but are often floating masses of peat.

At 1.2 miles cross a wooden bridge spanning Egypt Meadow Lake. To your left, on a point that juts out into the lake, is one of two primitive camping areas at Bruce Lake. The southern arm of the lake opens a clear view of Balsam Swamp to the right.

Across the bridge the difference in topography is severe. Atop a rise of less than 70 feet rocks and boulders strew the forest floor. On the left at 2 miles, a long rock shelf 20 feet high suddenly changes the level of the forest. Caves pierce the shelf—many large enough to shelter humans, bear, or bobcat. A shaggy grey fox trotted casually across the road into the boulder-strewn area near the shelf, looked my way without concern, and disappeared into the tangle of rocks and underbrush.

At 2.4 miles, leave the woods road and join the yellow-blazed West Branch Bruce Lake Trail to the right (south), along the western edge of Bruce Lake and the southern end of Balsam Swamp. (Down Bruce Lake Road .5 mile further, the East Branch Bruce Lake Trail heads right—south—along the east side of the lake. The two trails join in 1.3 miles.)

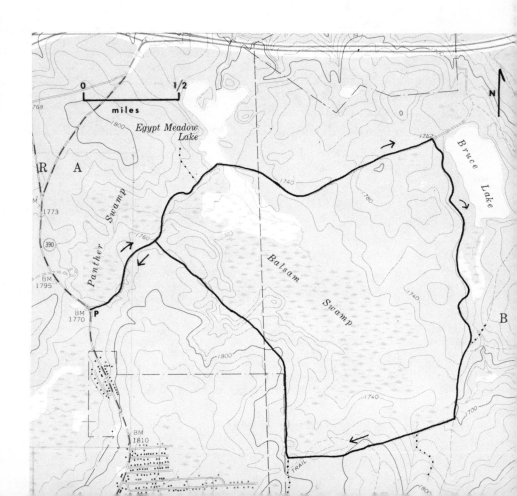

178 *Northern Tier and the Pocono Plateau*

The narrow West Branch Bruce Lake Trail winds through thick underbrush of laurel and raspberries that will scratch anyone foolish enough to wear shorts. Mosquitoes are fierce wherever the trail takes you closer to the lake. At 3 miles Bruce Lake is no longer open water but swamp—and the trail, wet and thorny. Near the south end of the lake, two adult Canada geese and their six half-grown offspring loudly upbraided four deer splashing through the swamp.

At 3.7 miles the East Branch Bruce Lake Trail comes in from the left. Continue due south, and at 4 miles cross swampy Shohola Creek. Drowned trees here have long since rotted, leaving large open areas that look like meadow from a distance. Close up, you see that grass springs from the water, frequently only inches deep. Clear water runs only in the stream channel, and patches of dry land dot the swamp. Further south, the trail dries out and crosses small hills of dense blueberry and laurel bushes. Beyond Shohola Creek you climb 200 feet in 1 mile along broad Rock Oak Ridge.

At 5 miles reach a trail intersection and turn right onto well-marked Rock Oak Ridge Trail. After a series of turns near the beginning, the slightly damp and rocky trail heads west. At 6.1 miles, the trail loops around several abandoned trails; at 6.5 miles the Rock Oak Ridge Trail seems to end at a **T**. Several trails diverge here, and the state park and United States Geological Survey maps differ somewhat. Be sure to turn right here onto the Brown Trail—the clearest path. In 100 yards come to a clearing where the Brown Trail again bears right. (Straight ahead leads to a telephone company building at the edge of Promised Land.)

The well-worn Brown Trail soon turns rocky and follows the wire-fenced boundary line of Promised Land. In another .4 mile the boundary wire angles west as you continue north. You'll have few views of Balsam Swamp, now on your right, and no trails lead down to the swamp. The rocks end at 7.2 miles and walking is pleasant to Bruce Lake Road at 7.8 miles. Turn left at the southeast edge of Panther Swamp and retrace your steps .5 mile to your car. Bruce Lake would make an excellent ski or snowshoe trip in winter, and fall hiking, after the first frost, brings relief from mosquitoes and leafless views into the swamps.

Bear Wallow Run Trail

Total distance: 2.2 miles
Hiking time: 1 hour
Vertical rise: 95 feet
Maps: USGS 7½' Promised Land; state park map

This short circuit hike in Promised Land State Park east of Scranton is near enough to Bruce Lake Natural Area (see Hike 43) to have some of the same features without the distance. Try this hike if you are a first-time hiker unprepared for an 8-mile hike, or if you'd like a quiet walk through interesting woods and bogs but haven't much time. You should see wildlife, and you may even see one of the trail's namesakes.

To reach the trailhead take I-84 to exit 7, then south on PA 390. Continue 1.3 miles to a pulloff on the right, where a gate bars entrance. If you are approaching from the west, drive east on I-80 to I-380, turn north following I-380 for 3 miles to PA 940, and turn east. In 6 miles, turn north (left) on PA 191, and right on PA 390 in 1 mile. Follow PA 390 north for 16 miles. If you're staying at a Promised Land State Park camp-ground, drive north on PA 390, pass-ing the entrance to Bruce Lake on the right. The trailhead for this hike will then be on the left, .2 mile beyond the Bruce Lake trailhead. Park by the gate.

Start hiking west down the road beyond the gate, the Bear Wallow Run Trail. The dirt two-track with grass between the ruts is easy walking, used in winter for snowmobiling. Almost immediately the

Kleinhans Trail, your return route, comes in from the right. Continue straight ahead, passing a small swamp on the right. Most of this hike is along dry ground through mature pines, maples, and beeches, with views into small swamps from the small hill on which you're walking. In this area of eastern Pennsylvania, *hill* refers to any piece of land that's even a few feet above a swamp.

Promised Land State Park has a local reputation for having nearly as many bears as people. Bear tracks in muddy areas are common sights; in the campground I'd seen several bears foraging for food. At .3 mile, heading down a slight hill I saw a small bear in the distance, probably a yearling abandoned in the spring when its mother had another cub. But a small bear is still a large animal: this one weighed about 100 pounds. The cub watched me with interest for a few seconds in a staring contest, then turned and hurried away off the trail. This was an exciting encounter—my first meeting with a bear in the wild. But this cub could have been one that I had already seen at the campground, only 1.5 miles south of the Bear Wallow Run Trail, as the bear walks.

Continue downhill, then uphill slightly.

Directly south at .6 mile is a small swamp, more of a bog than the wide, extensive Panther and Balsam swamps just east of PA 390 in the Bruce Lake Natural Area. If you venture off the trail down to the swamp edged with hemlocks and a few white pines, you'll see the deep cinna-mon-colored swamp water, dis-colored by tannic acid leaching into the water and soil from the hemlocks and pines. The natural pollutant makes water unfit to drink, but in the eighteenth and nineteenth centuries hemlock bark was a common source of tannin for tanning leather. Today, in northern Michigan and Wisconsin there is so mucn tannic acid in the spring runoff that streams and rivers run red. Here, the streams show no visible evidence of the substance, but wherever water is not flowing, a swamp or bog, the discoloration is noticeable.

At .8 mile come to a trail intersection. The Bear Wallow Run Trail continues ahead, climbing 100 feet to Big Dam Ridge where it intersects Bear Wallow Trail and curves toward the park campgrounds. For the intersection, the two trails with easily confused names follow roughly parallel routes south. Instead, turn right (north) at the inter-section onto the Panther Trail, which stays on high ground, narrow and inaccessible to winter snowmobilers.

At 1.3 miles begin to notice a small swamp on your right through the trees. The trail skirts the wet area, a depression about 20 feet lower than the surrounding woods. No stream leads into the area to

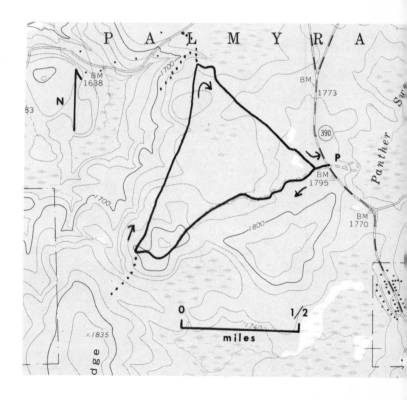

supply it with water, as Bear Wallow Run feeds the swamp south of the Bear Wallow Run Trail. In fact, the surrounding ridges effectively stop any streams from emptying into this area. The answer must be a spring somewhere in the dark water among fallen logs.

The Panther Trail heads uphill slightly, then downhill, and reaches an inter-section at 1.5 miles. Turn right onto the Kleinhans Trail, another woods road used by snowmobilers. (If you turn left you will come to paved Old Greentown Road in .25 mile, just beyond where the Bear Wallow Trail to the left ends.) The Kleinhans Trail eventually returns you to the Bear Wallow Run Trail, completing the three-trail loop just a short distance from your car.

The road winds around to another small swampy area at 1.8 miles; unless you're hiking in early spring you won't even get your feet wet. Bullfrogs, as well as those with less imposing voices, make their presence known and raccoon tracks crisscross the mud at the edge. Another hiker told me that this little swamp was lush with wildflowers in early spring —even more numerous and varied than those in Bruce Lake Natural Area, he claimed.

At 2.1 miles turn left onto Bear Wallow Run trail and retrace your steps .1 mile to the gate where you parked. You could easily lengthen you hike by using other trails that loop through Promised Land State Park, including the Bear Wallow Trail that leads southeast back to the park campground.

Wallenpaupack Creek

Total distance: 3.25 miles
Hiking time: 1½ hours
Vertical rise: 50 feet
Maps: USGS 7½' Promised Land; state park map

This pretty trek in Promised Land State Park follows East Branch Wallenpaupack Creek through cool hemlock woods where waterfalls splash over boulders into the creek. The area is excellent for observing wildlife: I watched a family of beavers at close range and discovered their well-disguised home in the creekbank. Children, especially, love water and wildlife, and under close supervision among the rocks should find this an easy walk.

East Branch Wallenpaupack Creek is just south of the wetlands of Bruce Lake Natural Area and Bear Wallow Run Trail (see Hikes 43 and 44). To reach Lower Lake Campground and the trailhead, take exit 7 off I-84 east of Scranton. Drive 4.7 miles south on PA 390. The creek is another 2 miles to the right down Lower Lake Road. From the south take I-80 to I-380, between exits 43 and 44. Follow I-380 north 4 miles to PA 940 east. Drive 8 miles east to Paradise Valley, where you turn north on PA 191. Drive 4 miles and bear right on PA 390 at Mountainhome. Continue north on PA 390 for 15 miles to Promised Land State Park. Turn left at the park office onto Lower Lake Road and drive 2 miles to Wallenpaupack Creek. Cross the bridge over the creek and reach the campground registration booth in the middle of the road. Park near the booth.

Begin walking downstream on the east side of the creek. In 100 yards, cross a wooden footbridge to the west side of the creek, and immediately turn right on an unmarked trail. You will hike the west bank downstream on the East Branch Wallenpaupack Trail, returning to your car on the east bank.

Wallenpaupack Creek flows out of Lower Lake northwest into privately-owned Lake Paupack, following a narrow ravine between two hills. Both banks are densely forested with mature hemlocks, cool and breezy in the hottest weather. Flat chunks of slate line the peaty floor. The slate is usually wet—and slippery where the trail follows the edge of the creek closely. Arrowhead, low-growing ferns, and seedlings of beech and hickory line the streambanks.

About .25 mile from the trailhead, I saw a young beaver the size of a muskrat, calmly chewing a seedling on the opposite bank of the 15-foot creek. Although it saw me, the beaver swam across the stream toward me and clambered out onto the bank only 5 feet away. It nibbled some small plants, then waddled back to the stream and swam

away. The young beaver was too small to be on its own, unless it had been abandoned; the beaver family and the dam had to be nearby.

At .4 mile reach Little Falls, a pretty cascade dropping 8 feet over boulders in the stream. At .5 mile the topography opens from rocky shale under dense hemlocks to a less densely forested area of beeches, maples, and tall grass. Footprints of raccoons and birds are easy to identify here in the sandy soil. In early spring, high water loaded with sediment floods this wide flat section, depositing the sandy soil, possibly from the lake bottom.

To the right a bridge crosses to the east side of the creek. For this hike continue .7 mile along the creek to where the trail ends at the state forest boundary. You will backtrack to this bridge to return on the east bank of the creek. Beyond the bridge and small cascading waterfalls, the land retains its grassy openness. Downstream, as you near Lake Paupack, the hills grow more rounded and the stream broadens and moves more slowly.

At 1.2 miles East Branch Wallen-

paupack Trail ends. Retrace your steps .7 mile back to the bridge and cross to explore the east bank of the creek. Walking is easier on this side, on the wide band of flat land between the surrounding hills and the creek, carpeted with swamp maples, grasses, and ferns. I saw a raccoon and fresh tracks, and a tree destroyed by woodpeckers, now housing a family of sparrows—but I looked in vain for more signs of beaver.

About 200 yards across the bridge, the flat belt widens into a small meadow. Trees are down in places, from high water or wind but bearing no scars of beaver activity. At the south edge of this clearing I sighted the beaver family—two babies and their huge mother—her tail the size of a rug beater. The mother seemed unconcerned by my presence, allowing me to approach quite close. The family slowly cut down saplings, preferring low beech trees and branches the thickness of a pencil, and finally ambled down to the water. The mother beaver, holding a 3-foot limb in her mouth, headed upstream.

Problems surfaced—what direction to go and how to navigate the stick around

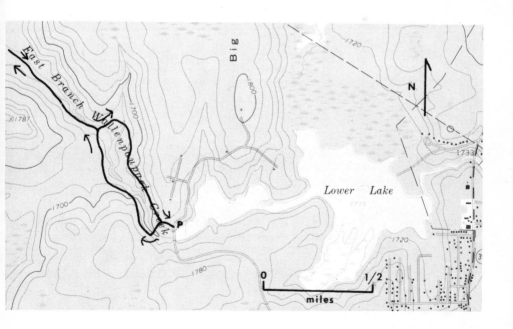

rocks. After several false starts and changes of direction, the young beavers gave up trying to help and started playing in the water—climbing onto their mother's tail or back, crying if she got too far ahead of them. Soon both young beavers were crying continuously. The female climbed slowly up the bank and rolled onto her back, allowing the two to nurse.

Later, I followed the beavers to their home—a hole on the streambank where a large hemlock grew on a curve in the stream. Water had eroded the soil from the roots, creating a 3-foot hollow that provided ample quarters for the family. Most of the beavers' activity seemed to take place between .25 and .4 mile from your parking spot. If you're hiking with children, you could shorten the hike by walking to the first bridge at .5 mile, crossing to return on the east bank.

The creek curves several times as you return to your car, but there are fewer stones on this side, and less chance of slipping or falling into the creek. Reach the wooden footbridge at 3.2 miles, and Lower Lake Road and your car in 100 yards. From local rangers, I found that observation of beavers at close range is a typical experience for visitors to Promised Land State Park. Many animals (beavers, raccoons, deer, bear) have lost much of their fear of man—a fact considerably more appealing about beavers than bears.

Blooming Grove 4-H Trail

Total distance: 3.3 miles
Hiking time: 1 ¾ hours
Vertical rise: 75 feet
Map: USGS 7 ½' Hawley

There must be more blueberry bushes per square foot along this hike in Pike County north of Promised Land State Park than anywhere else in eastern Pennsylvania. Hikers will find a varied topography of meadow, forest, and swamp—and a feast of ripe blueberries in July. You will follow only one loop of this 6.5-mile hiking trail of loops and connecting trails built by 4-H'ers near Lake Wallenpaupack, to make it easier to return to your car.

To reach the trailhead, take I-84 to exit 8, about 30 miles east of Scranton. Turn north (left) onto PA 402. In 4.5 miles pass the road to White Deer Lake on the right, and at 5 miles, reach a dirt road on the left. Turn downhill for 100 yards to the ample parking lot, shown on maps as a gravel pit.

Follow the well-worn path at the southwest end of the parking area to the red-blazed Blooming Grove Trail, which begins where the path enters the woods on your right, at the edge of the power-line cut. Before entering the woods you might see a few blazes on large rocks, and in the forest the red blazes sometimes blend into the tree bark on a sunless day. But once you are through the tangle of rocks, underbrush, and poison ivy at the forest's

edge, you won't have any trouble following the trail.

Follow the path south through an unusual and very pretty forest of large clumps of graceful white birches scattered throughout the forest floor of sometimes waist-high grass. This bright green and white woods with spaced trees seems more like a park or overgrown meadow than a forest; in fact, further south you'll reach the area called Gates Meadow. Although Gates Meadow is actually on the edge of a swamp, it looks as though it should be filled with grazing Holsteins.

At .5 mile, the topography changes from meadowlike forest to the kind of swamp in Bruce Lake Natural Area (see Hike 43). This swamp is much smaller than Panther or Balsam swamps, but here also are gaunt skeletons of dead trees and abundant wildlife. The smaller size and the way the trail passes the swamp here make it easier for hikers and birders to observe. You may want to bring your binoculars and take a break from hiking to spend some time watching the swamp. A general rule: you'll see more wildlife by sitting still than by walking.

Many animals thrive equally well in both

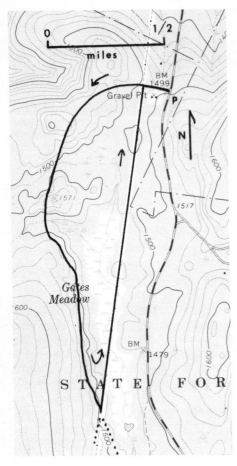

worn. At .6 mile, the trail gains a few feet of elevation—enough to cross a section of dry land, temporarily leaving the swamp behind. I hiked here in an unseasonably dry year, so you could expect wetter conditions in spring or in a year of more rainfall. If you attempt the trail then, you'll need good footwear; leather hiking boots work well if you waterproof them properly and allow them to dry out after your hike. Wear long pants, even in hot weather; they'll protect you from mosquitoes and heavy underbrush—which frequently hides poison ivy.

At 1 mile, a slight descent brings you to the next swampy section. In the swamps, only inches deep, the predominant plants are grass and bushes of vines and weeds. But the life of the swamp is most visible overhead in the dead and dying trees. I saw an indigo bunting, rufous-sided towhees, red-winged blackbirds, a sparrow hawk, a red-tailed hawk, several goldfinches, and many others—and I heard many more birds than I saw.

Beyond the wet area walk along the sides of Gates Hill, still heading south parallel to Gates Meadow. At 1.75 miles, reach the power-line cut you saw when you began your hike. The Blooming Grove Trail continues south across the cut, reaching Grassy Road in .5 mile. At that intersection a left turn takes you to PA 402 in .4 miles; a right turn takes you south to the village of Blooming Grove in about 3 miles.

But if the thought of blueberry pie or sweet, wild blueberries makes your mouth water, you'll turn left at the power-line cut and follow it north back to your car. At 2 miles reach a small wet area, which soon dries out, and you'll find yourself surrounded by blueberry bushes. Prime blueberry season in an average year is July; some berries may be ready the first week, but you'll be able to pick more and larger berries by the end of the month. The combination of sandy soil and sunlight

swamp and forest—rabbits, turtles, and deer—but some birds definitely prefer swampy areas. Hawks perch on dead branches to scout prey, preferring the openness of the swamp to the cover of the forest. Flickers and downy and red-bellied woodpeckers, found in almost any forest, seem more numerous in swamps, where they feed on insects under the bark of swamp-killed trees. I watched a belted kingfisher look for its dinner of small minnows in the swamp.

Downed trees and brush along the trail might obscure your path in this swampy area, where the path itself is not much

brought by the power-line cut to this normally forested area produces some fantastic berries.

A good way to harvest blueberries while you're hiking is to cut holes into the sides of an empty coffee tin at the top. Loop some rope through the holes and carry the can around your neck. This leaves your hands free while you're hiking, and gives you two hands to harvest berries. The most enticing berries in these waist-high blueberry bushes always seem to be in the middle of the bush, between stones and poison ivy.

The power-line cut returns you to the parking area at the gravel pit at 3.3 miles. If you're more interested in berrying than hiking, you can park here and walk south along the power-line cut .5 mile to the best blueberry section of the hike.

Backpacks

Stony Creek Valley Abandoned RR

Time allowed: 2 days, 1 night
Total distance: 18 miles
Vertical rise: 400 feet
Maps: USGS 15' Harrisburg, USGS 15' Hummelstown,
USGS 15' Lykens; state forest map; K.T.A. 4

Just north of Dauphin and Harrisburg, this two-day backpack follows the long-abandoned Schuylkill and Susquenhanna Railroad bed through some of the wildest mountains and one of the largest roadless areas in eastern Pennsylvania. Now a maintenance road for State Game Lands 211, the railroad bed parallels Stony Creek through the narrow valley bounded by Sharp and Stony mountains to the north and Second Mountain to the south. Stony Creek Valley averages only .5 mile wide, but is over 20 miles long, with no passable road to mar its isolation.

The hike is one-way, requiring two cars: one at the trailhead just past Ellendale Forge near White Spring, east of Dauphin, and a second car on Gold Mine Road at the end of the hike. Now a good dirt road, the nearly-flat railroad bed is not hard enough to hurt your feet even if you walk the entire distance in a single day, definitely feasible for well-conditioned hikers. For those who prefer a slower pace, the only spot where camping is permissible is the Rausch Gap shelter 1 mile north of the railroad grade on the Appalachian Trail (AT)—14 miles from the trailhead. The second day's hike is

shorter—4 miles. If you hike the whole distance in one day, the total from Ellendale Forge to Gold Mine Road is 16 miles.

To spot a car on Gold Mine Road at the end of the hike, take US 22—US 322 north from Harrisburg. Turn right on PA 443 at Fort Hunter, 2 miles south of Dauphin. Stay on PA 443 for 20 miles, past Green Point along Swatara Creek. Gold Mine Road turns left off PA 443 and immediately heads up Second Mountain. Drive 3.8 miles on Gold Mine Road, passing two dirt roads on the left, to the bridge at Evening Branch Creek. Turn left on the road just before the bridge and continue .8 mile to a roadblock where you can leave a car.

To spot a second car, return to US 22—US 322, turning right into Dauphin. Soon after entering town, cross a bridge over Stony Creek and immediately turn right on a road parallel to the creek. Continue 6 miles, following signs to the game lands. The road turns from pavement to dirt, then narrows and ends at another gate with plenty of parking space. Access in winter or in a muddy spring might prove difficult on the final stretch of dirt road.

Day 1

Ellendale Forge to Rausch Gap
Total distance: 14 miles
Hiking time: 6½ hours
Vertical rise: 400 feet

Begin walking around the gate east on the road you drove in on, now blocked to traffic. Your route is almost perfectly flat and straight—except for the steep climb up Sharp Mountain to the shelter at Rausch Gap. Beyond the first mile you aren't likely to see other hikers in this remote area. The steep hill on the left is forested with mature oak, hickory, and tulip poplar, with little underbrush except laurel. In winter, you can see nearly to the top of the mountain from the railroad bed. To the right is hemlock-shrouded Stony Creek where the laurel is thicker and wetland plants such as skunk cabbage and violets abound in low-lying stretches near the creek.

Most of the road crosses State Game Lands 211 so you should hike only on Sundays here during hunting seasons. Feed stands along your route—barrels stocked with corn and hay by the Pennsylvania Game Commission—help see the deer and turkey populations through the winter. Several gauging stations along the creek test water flow and depth. If you leave the path to walk 25 feet down to the creek, keep a close lookout in the underbrush for rattlesnakes, prevalent in this area. On the trail itself you'll be able to see a snake long before you reach biting range.

Near an open spot on the left at 2 miles the Water Tank Trail leads uphill on a rough, steep path over Sharp Mountain to the Stony Mountain Fire Tower. Beyond the intersection .8 mile is Metropolitan Edison land, where the road may be deeply rutted in wet seasons by the utility company's heavy equipment. Atop the rock-strewn mountain to the left is an old stagecoach trail that heads through St.

Anthonys Wilderness (see Hike 23). The railroad was built after the stagecoach line, connecting the eastern part of the state with places further west. Today the area is wilder than it was when horses clattered along the mountain ridge, and iron horses belched smoke in the valley.

At 6.5 miles the Horseshoe Trail comes in from the left, down the mountain on one of the easier grades. An extended horseback riding and hiking trail, the Horseshoe Trail begins here atop the mountain and runs southeast all the way to Valley Forge, following the old railroad grade 2.5 miles, then heading off to the right. Through this section a chorus of frogs will accompany you through lush ferns, and animals frequently cross your path: turtles, rabbits, deer, red fox. This remote area is well known for ruffed grouse in hunting season, and occasionally someone even shoots a coyote or hears a bobcat—sightings that indicate what a quiet and lucky hiker might encounter.

When you reach Yellow Springs Trail on the left at 9.5 miles, Fort Indiantown Gap will be to the south, across Second Mountain. Yellow Springs Trail leads north into the heart of St. Anthonys Wilderness and the area where the stagecoach stop Yellow Springs Village was once situated.

If you hike in spring you may see the most unusual use of the old Schuylkill and Susquehanna bed—spring sled dog training. When there's no snow, sled dog fanciers hook their teams to three-wheeled aluminum chariots. One early spring morning I saw five different teams of young dogs on the flat, wide road. The abandoned railroad also makes an excellent cross-country ski tour in winter. Even a novice skier could probably make the entire distance, with no hills to negotiate. If driving back on a snow-covered road to the gate is a problem, there are places to park along

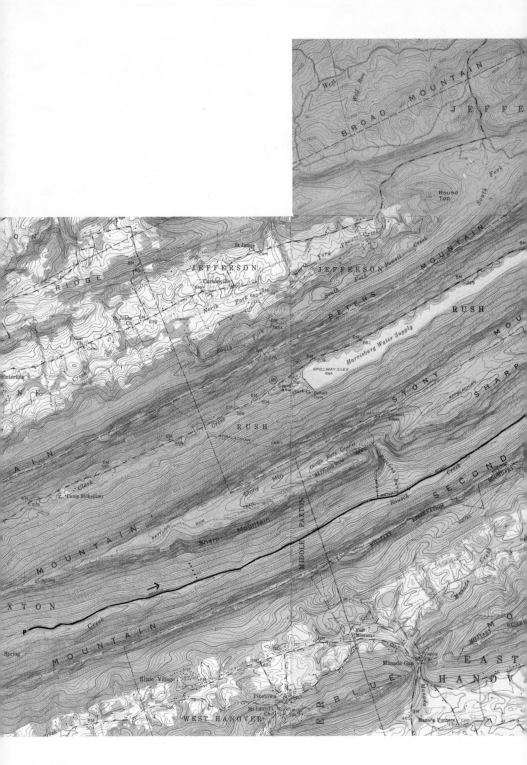

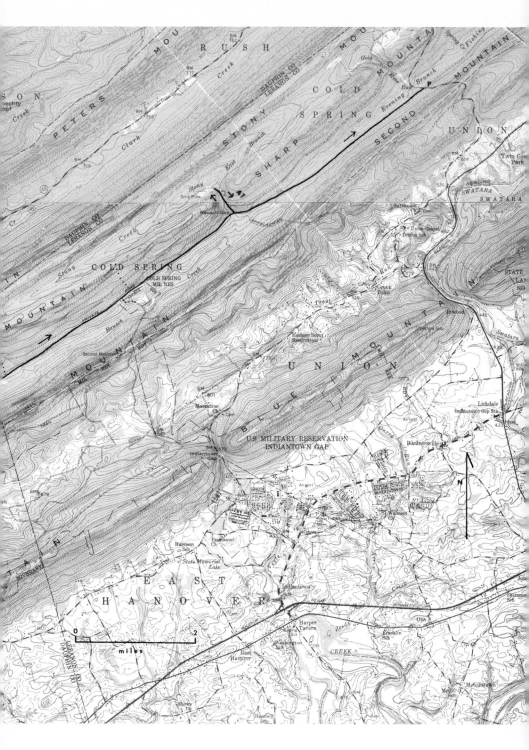

the road, which would add another mile or so to the trip.

At 13 miles reach the intersection of the Appalachian Trail; turn left to follow the creek 500 feet up Rausch Gap, a steep climb after a long day's hiking. Near the very top of the mountain is Rausch Gap Shelter, a small lean-to accommodating four hikers. The creek tumbling out of the gap is known locally as Rausch Creek, although it is a part of Stony Creek and also called that on some maps. For photographers the rocky, pretty gap and creek are an extra bonus of the hike, especially with sunlight streaming through the hemlocks.

Day 2
Rausch Gap to Gold Mine Road
Total distance: 4 miles
Hiking time: 1¾ hours
Vertical rise: minimal

Since the second day's hike out to Gold Mine Road is so short, you could explore the Rausch Gap area before heading for home. A good way is to continue on the Appalachian Trail for a short distance as it heads along Sharp Mountain. Unless you're an experienced woodsman or woodswoman, you shouldn't leave the trail; the area is extremely isolated and becoming turned around is easy. Bushwhacking is also likely to bring out snakes in spring and summer, and they're harder to avoid in the underbrush.

When you decide to head home, retrace your steps down Rausch Gap on the AT, reaching the abandoned railroad bed in 1 mile. Turn left and continue on the path, now only 3 miles from your car. At 1.5 miles reach the swampy headwaters of Stony Creek. Your path continues through the valley, still flat and easy walking.

Although your hike ends at the gate where you spotted a car, the railroad bed continues to Lebanon Reservoir, 2 miles northeast beyond Gold Mine Road—a pretty morning or afternoon hike in itself. If you're still not ready to return home, you could toss your overnight gear in the car and walk to the end of the line, extending your second day's hike to 8 miles, 4 miles without a pack.

Conestoga Trail

Time allowed: 2 days, 1 night
Total distance: 15 miles
Vertical rise: 2,200 feet
Maps: USGS 7½' Conestoga, USGS 7½' Holtwood;
Conestoga Trail map

The rugged 15-mile Conestoga Trail built by the Lancaster Hiking Club in southern Lancaster County follows the eastern rim of the cliffs overlooking the Susquehanna River, often 300 feet above water level. Views of the mile-wide river and its forested shoreline are spectacular and almost continuous. For most of the hike you'll be far removed from the nearest road, high above feeding waterfowl below you on rocky outcroppings in the Susquehanna.

If you're in excellent condition, you might be able to hike the Conestoga Trail in a single day, but two days will give you time to take note of your surroundings. You won't have to get an early start your first day out because the only campsite is just 5.7 miles into the hike. Camping is not permitted elsewhere along the trail, which is primarily on Pennsylvania Power and Light Company land. Spring and fall are ideal seasons for this hike, avoiding the heat of the summer as well as snakes and ticks. One short section of the trail crosses State Game Lands 288 where hunting is permitted. Maps are available from George Aukamp, Lake Aldred Supt., Pennsylvania Power and Light Co., Holtwood, PA 17532 (717-284-2278).

The Conestoga Trail is not a loop, so you will need to spot cars at both ends of the hike: one at Lock 12 Historic Area 25 miles southeast of York, a second car at the north end of the trail at Martic Forge in southern Lancaster County. The hike described runs from north to south, but there is no reason why you couldn't hike the other direction depending on your easiest access. The main consideration is the campsite 5.7 miles from the north trailhead, whether to hike the shorter distance the first day or the second.

If you are driving from York, you can easily spot the first car at Lock 12, a canal lock on the now abandoned Susquehanna Canal in York County. Drive southeast from York 22 miles on PA 74 until you reach PA 372, turn left, and in 2 miles reach the Susquehanna River. Turn left just before the Norman Wood Bridge and reach the Lock 12 Historic Area parking lot in .1 mile.

To spot a second car at the northern end of the hike at Martic Forge, head back out to PA 372, turn left across the Susquehanna, and continue 2 miles to Bethesda. Turn left on River Road, north toward Martic Forge. In 4 miles the River Road passes Mount Nebo Cemetery on the left. Here, bear right, then left in .5 mile, reaching Martic Forge 2.5 miles

beyond. Park in a pulloff on the left where the road ends.

From Lancaster you can reach Martic Forge by driving south 14 miles on PA 324. From Martic Forge, the rest of your driving directions will be reversed—continue to Holtwood on River Road before joining PA 372 to spot the second car at Lock 12.

Day 1
Martic Forge to Reed Run
Total distance: 5.7 miles
Hiking time: 3 hours
Vertical rise: 700 feet

The orange-blazed Conestoga Trail heads south on the paved River Road for .1 mile, beginning at Martic Forge. Where the road bends left, follow the trail to the right, along the edge of Pequea (pronounced Peck-way) Creek to where it empties into the Susquehanna, a total of 3.7 miles. For the first 1.5 miles you'll follow the edge of State Game Lands 288, through thick woods of oak and tulip poplar, with hemlocks and pines hugging the creek banks. Hunting is permitted here, except on Sundays, so you should either avoid hiking during hunting season altogether, or wear a protective orange cap, especially on the first day of small game or deer season. You also might want to avoid hiking on the opening day of trout season, when large numbers of anglers arrive at the creek.

From here to the Susquehanna River your trail is wide and flat—the old abandoned Pequea trolly bed. At 1.3 miles the trail crosses a road, edging the Pequea Creek Recreation Area on the left until 2.6 miles. This year-round campground (water and toilets available), or the Otter Creek Recreation Area on the York County side of the Susquehanna, would make a good base for hiking in this area (see Hikes 17, 18, and 19), but the campground fills with hunters or

fishermen during the early days of those seasons.

The trail soon swings south in a wide arc along the creek. Squirrels and chipmunks dart back and forth scolding a group of hikers or a blue jay, cardinal, or chickadee that ventures too close. Beginning at 2.6 miles pass several trail intersections on the left, part of the nature trail system along the boundary of the recreation area. These interesting side trails head uphill away from the creek, then loop back to the Conestoga Trail in less than 1 mile. Just beyond the trail intersections, you'll cross a 1-mile-long section of privately owned forest outside the town of Pequea. As Pequea Creek turns toward the Susquehanna, the trail bends to the right (west) through a large stand of mature oaks.

At 3.7 miles reach Pequea, a Susquehanna river town on the south side of Pequea Creek. The trail heads west on a town street for .1 mile, then turns south again, paralleling another road for a short distance before beginning an uphill pull to the top of the bluffs. You climb steadily but slowly, soon with river views on the right. Upriver is Weise Island; across are high, rocky Urey Lookout and the Urey Islands just offshore. The opposite bank is the Otter Creek Recreation Area, with steep, rocky cliffs and forested hills straight down to the river's edge. The sheer cliffs, along with the threat of floods, have kept development of the river shore at a minimum, although you'll be able to see a few summer homes.

At 4.1 miles the trail heads off the hill temporarily, dropping 300 feet in .2 mile. At the bottom cross three roads, all within .1 mile of each other. You won't cross another road until tomorrow when you reach Holtwood, about 6 miles south. At 4.1 miles reach Wind Cave, a rock outcropping with another spectacular river view. Bair Island and several islands to the south are gathering points for waterfowl: Canada geese, herring gulls

that fly up from Chesapeake Bay to feed, herons and egrets in summer. During the spring and fall migrations you can see flocks of whistling swans and snow geese heading up or down the river.

Beyond Wind Cave lookout the leaves of summer may obscure the view somewhat, but you're rarely out of sight of the river. Cross narrow, rocky House Rock Run at 5 miles, then turn first right, then left uphill to House Rock at 5.1 miles. The low, rocky outcrop islands, Duncan Island south and Bair Island across the river, are populated only by river birds.

Continue past House Rock on top of the bluffs, crossing Brubaker Run at 5.3 miles and narrow, boulder-filled Reed Run at 5.5 miles. The trail heads uphill and turns right (west) to reach the primitive campsite where you will spend the night. Although it looks lovely and clear, the water from Reed Run should be boiled if you don't carry in your own.

Day 2
Reed Run to Lock 12
Total distance: 9.3 miles
Hiking time: 5 hours
Vertical rise: 1,500 feet

Most of today's hike follows the very edge of the river, off the top of the bluffs. There is a definite wilderness feeling here as you hike to several rocky overlooks with excellent views, then descend through small stream glens filled with magnificent trees and large boulders. This morning you follow Reed Run downstream (southwest) .2 mile through large hemlocks with little underbrush. When you reach the Susquehanna, turn left (southeast) with the bluffs above you on the left.

Railroad tracks line the very edge of the river, a good place to drop your backpack and head down to the shoreline to explore. The edge of the river is rocky, lined with

almost perfectly rounded small stones. Before the Civil War, the river was used for running logs. Later, coal barges plied the waters, but the Susquehanna was never deep enough to be considered navigable. Now dams regulate water levels up and down its length, some of them part of a hydroelectric system, like the one you'll see further south. Although the river is usually only several feet deep, during flooding it sometimes triples its depth and runs well over its banks.

Leave the riverbank and continue southeast on the Conestoga Trail. At 1.2 miles the trail crosses Tucquan Creek, leaves the river's edge, and climbs again to the bluffs, gaining 300 feet in .2 mile. From an unnamed rocky overlook, another tiny island— Hartman Island—is directly ahead. Further out toward the western shore is Reed Island. South is Lake Aldred Gorge, a narrow section of the Susquehanna deepened to 190 feet at a bend by Holtwood Dam 3.5 miles to the south.

Beyond the overlook head back toward the river again, losing the 300 feet of elevation less rapidly than the ascent. At 2.2 miles reach Pinnacle Overlook, one of the most panoramic views on the Conestoga Trail (water and toilets available). From this point you'll follow part of the route described as a day hike in Kellys Run Natural Area (see Hike 17). At 2.4 miles the trail heads downhill from an overlook at a power-line cut. To the south are the Holtwood power plant and dam. At Kellys Run turn left upstream away from the river, reaching Holtwood Recreation Area at 4.4 miles (about 1.5 miles east of the Susquehanna).

The trail bends southwest from here to return to the river. Cross a road at 4.9 miles along a power-line cut, passing just east of the town of Holtwood at 5.6 miles, where you cross another road. The trail loses altitude steadily now, paralleling a road. At 6.2 miles cross a series of power lines

and reach Face Rock Overlook with views of Piney Island just ahead, and Brushy, Wildcat, and Crow islands, and the Norman Wood Bridge on PA 372 to the south. The difference in the river below the dam can be dramatic: in some seasons most of the river channel is exposed and dry with just a few inches to a foot of water trickling between the rocks.

From the overlook the trail continues downhill, then more directly south, still above river level. Just before reaching PA 372, at 7.2 miles the trail heads sharply downhill again. Turn right on PA 372 across the Norman Wood Bridge, reaching the opposite bank at 8.9 miles. Here the trail proceeds downhill to the right, turning right again at 9.1 miles, then left, ending at 9.3 miles total at your car. The Lock 12 Historic Area is located here, and you can visit what remains of the old lock on the now fragmented Susquehanna Canal.

Caledonia to Pine Grove Furnace

Time allowed: 2 days, 1 night
Total distance: 19.1 miles
Vertical rise: 1,750 feet
*Maps: USGS 7½' Caledonia, USGS 7½' Walnut Bottom, USGS 7½'
Dickinson; P.A.T.C. #2, #3; state forest map*

The Appalachian Trail (AT) through
Michaux State Forest west of the
Susquehanna climbs old woods roads
through hills lined by tree-sized
rhododendron and mountain laurel. On
the ridge of South Mountain you'll pass
dozens of huge anthills, reaching the Big
Flat fire tower midway for a panoramic
view of endless mountains and
agricultural Cumberland Valley. A stiff
climb or two—with descents along wild,
rushing streams—make this backpack
strenuous enough to be interesting, suited
for all but the first-time backpacker or the
hottest summer weekend. A winter's hike
would avoid the heat and sweat generated
on a humid day, and offer vistas
unencumbered by leafy growth.

Camping will be at the two Birch Run
shelters, each sleeping four hikers. Mice
abound in both lean-tos, however, and if
your hiking party is small, you might pack
a tent to keep them out of your sleeping
bag—midnight mouse races around
weary hikers seem to be their favorite
sport. Since this isn't a circle hike, you'll
need to spot one car at Pine Grove
Furnace at the end of the hike, and another
at Caledonia State Park in lots where
overnight parking is allowed.

To spot a car at Pine Grove Furnace,
take US 30 west 15 miles from Gettysburg,
or 10 miles east from Chambersburg, to
Caledonia. From Harrisburg or further
north drive I-81 to Chambersburg, then
east on US 30 to Caledonia. When you turn
north on PA 233 at Caledonia, you reach
the entrance to Caledonia Park on the left
almost immediately. Pass the entrance
and trailhead for now and continue north
15 miles on PA 233. Just before reaching
Fuller Lake Recreation Area, pass a
wooden sign on the left showing the AT
intersection. As you continue ahead,
notice white AT blazes painted on
telephone poles on the right side of PA
233.

In .1 mile the blazes turn right onto a
side road, past a fine, old yellow brick
mansion, once the ironmaster's home,
sitting grandly on your left. Just beyond
the inn, a dirt road on the right brings you
within sight of Pine Grove Furnace (only a
brick chimney remains) where overnight
parking is allowed. Built about 1770, the
furnace operated under a succession of
owners until 1893, when the nearby ore
hole was flooded, forming Fuller Lake.
Just above the furnace were a grist mill
(now housing) and stables (now a state
park concession).

Return on PA 233 to Caledonia Park to

park your second car at the trailhead. Stop at the park office on the right just past the entrance to register your car to leave it overnight and receive parking information. You must drive all the way through the park, past the camping and picnic areas and swimming pool, to the end of the road where overnight parking is permitted. From the parking area you can see the white AT blazes at the edge of the picnic area where the mountain rises steeply.

Day 1
Caledonia to Birch Run
Total distance: 9 miles
Hiking time: 5½ hours
Vertical rise: 1,000 feet

Begin following the white blazes north up the mountain along a narrow wash, gaining 400 feet in .1 mile. After these strenuous first steps the climb evens somewhat to reach the top at .4 mile. The trail bears right onto the old woods road, Grove Ridge Road, across the top of Chinquapin Hill with views west to another ridge. At 1 mile pass Letterkenny Gun Club rifle range and turn right again on wide, dirt Green Road (passable by traffic). In .2 mile, the AT turns left, then left again on Quarry Gap Road at 1.4 miles. Giant, gnarled rhododendron over 8 feet high grow so thickly they block views on either side and threaten to choke the trail. Climb steadily, at 1.8 miles reaching the Quarry Gap shelters, built by the Civilian Conservation Corps in 1933, as were the Birch Run shelters. Beyond, follow the rocky stream on the right for a short distance before beginning the most severe climb of the hike—500 feet to the top at 2.4 miles.

Hiking on the ridge is fairly flat, through cool pines until you reach Sandy Sod, a junction of wide gravel roads at 3 miles. Follow the AT, well marked with wide blazes, across the intersection north. Just beyond Sandy Sod, you reach an AT trail registry where end-to-enders—hikers making the entire 2,054-mile trip from Springer Mountain, Georgia, to Mount Katahdin, Maine—sometimes leave messages: "Steve, I'll see you on Katahdin."

If you're using United States Geological Survey (USGS) maps, notice the colorful names of the geographical features around you: Devil Alex Hollow to the west, Stillhouse Hollow Road, Shirley Run, Dark Hollow to the southeast, and Wigwam Hill beyond. Mitten Hill is vaguely shaped like a mitten, and some of the names date from early ironworking years—Furnace Run, Quarry Gap. But most of the stories—of Devil Alex and Shirley—have been lost.

At 4 miles cross a power-line cut with good views north into an often swampy section. Just off the top of Big Pine Flat Ridge, the trail climbs and dips from hollow to hollow. At 4.4 miles cross Methodist Hill Road (impassable by car), descend to Sweigart Hollow, then climb into thick blueberries and mountain laurel. Laurel blooms with the rhododendron in June, with blueberries ready for hikers' lunches in July.

From here you will cross a series of woods roads: first Middle Ridge Road, then Old Dug Hill Road. At 6.3 miles cross Ridge Road again (the first time was at Sandy Sod), then Means Hollow and Canada Hollow roads. (A slightly shorter, easier way of reaching this point is to leave the AT at Sandy Sod, the 3-mile point, and follow Ridge Road to here. But you will miss the blueberries and almost continuous views of the mountains on the left.)

Past the intersection, the trail descends sharply to Milesburn Road and a locked AT cabin at 6.6 miles. Cross Milesburn Road and begin a steady climb over troublesome football-sized rocks that slow down tired hikers. At 6.9 miles cross

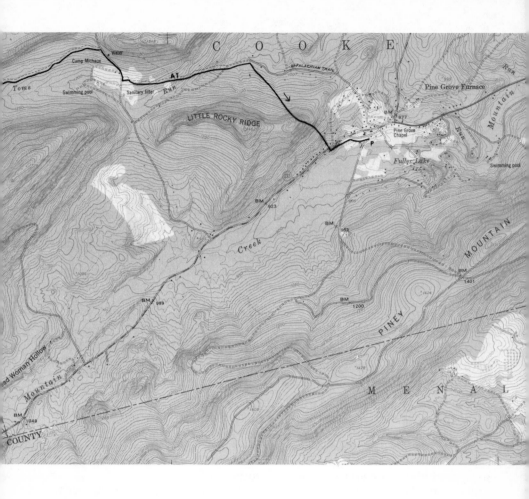

another road to enter a beautiful pine grove for .5 miles of easy and pretty walking. If you're very quiet you might see grouse or a wild turkey: I've heard turkeys call here, seen their tracks in snow and scratch marks on the ground in summer, but so far the bird itself has eluded me.

Beyond the pine grove cross an overgrown trail, pass under power lines, and reach Fegley Road at 8.3 miles. Continue ahead, passing the old AT as it winds around the current trail. Soon descend into a hollow, where at 9 miles you'll find the Birch Run shelters on the left and open areas for tents nearby. Water is available from the year-round stream.

Day 2
Birch Run to Pine Grove Furnace
Total distance: 10.1 miles
Hiking time: 5½ hours
Vertical rise: 750 feet

The second day of hiking is easier than the first: the elevation change is down, not up, and most of the descents are gradual. Cross Birch Run and head uphill to Big Flat at 1.1 miles. At 1.2 miles reach a paved road where you can leave the AT for a short, worthwhile side trip to the Big Flat fire tower. Turn left on the paved road and walk 200 feet to Ridge Road, turn right (east), and continue .25 mile. Here, a road to the left leads to the tower in 100 yards. The view from here is of one rolling mountain after another to the south, west, and east, with farmlands in the Cumberland Valley to the north. Return to the AT by backtracking along the fire tower route to the AT again at 1.8 miles.

On the AT you reach Dead Woman Hollow at 2.4 miles and Dead Woman Hollow Road at 2.8 miles. At 3.6 miles a blue-blazed trail leads right .2 mile to the locked Anna Michener Cabin, built by the Pennsylvania Appalachian Trail

Conference in 1963. The Tumbling Run loop (see Hike 30) passes by here, if you want to interweave trails.

Beyond the cabin, the forest shrinks to scrub—small trees and low shrubs—and you'll begin to see giant anthills built by armies of Allegheny mound-building ants. People who know the mountains here have told me that the large sand mounds—4 to 5 feet across, 3 feet high, and often less than 20 feet apart—were in the same places as long ago as fifty years. The ants seem to thrive on snacks tossed away by careless hikers—no reason to litter even if the ants do act like miniature garbagemen.

At 4.2 miles cross a gravel road and turn right at 5.3 miles. Almost devoid of large trees, the rocky section atop the flat supports only low shrubs in the dry, sandy, poor-quality soil. Fires have devastated this area, most recently in 1964, and occasional blackened stumps show the extent of the damage. The forest has been slow to regenerate, and the contrast between the nearly barren top and the verdant hills is striking. The open areas, however, seem to suit the ants, small birds in the low shrubs, and the small, sun-loving wildflowers in grassy spots.

Where the trail returns to more lush, but still sunny surroundings, I've seen the rare and endangered trailing arbutus with delicate, sweet-smelling white flowers—one of spring's earliest bloomers. The plant is hardly common here, but seems to be surviving, perhaps because forest officials are reluctant to tell visitors about it. Misguided amateur botanists have dug up the fragile arbutus in the mistaken belief they could grow it in home gardens.

At 5.6 miles cross Woodrow Road. From here, the general trend of the trail is ever downward, marking your descent toward Pine Grove Furnace. Head sharply downhill for 1 mile, then more gradually.

Cross Toms Run at 6 miles, reaching Toms Run shelters at 6.5 miles. The wide, frequently muddy trail here also accommodates raccoons, violets, Jack-in-the-pulpits, and tadpoles in the puddles.

At 7.6 miles reach High Mountain Road and turn right, following AT blazes. You soon pass the ruins of Camp Michaux, a children's summer camp until the 1970s. Before that it housed Civilian Conservation Corps workers, and German submarine personnel during World War II. The trail leaves the road at 7.8 miles, passing the stone ruins of the barn of the old Bunker Hill farm, where settlers are said to have been massacred by Indians.

At 8.5 miles reach the Pine Grove Furnace cabin, one of the earliest extant buildings of the region. Cross Toms Run again on the bridge and climb over a rough, rocky trail until 9.2 miles where the AT joins a narrow woods road. Turn right onto a wider gravel road at 9.8 miles and reach PA 233 at 9.9 miles. The Pine Grove store and furnace are .2 miles to the left—go along PA 233 for .1 mile, then right on the park road another .1 mile to reach your car.

50

Five Mountains

Time allowed: 4 days, 3 nights
Total distance: 40.4 miles
Vertical rise: 3,500 feet
Maps: USGS 15' New Bloomfield, USGS 15' Harrisburg,
   USGS 15' Hummelstown; K.T.A. 4;
   Darlington and Horseshoe trail maps

This rugged backpack for experienced hikers climbs, then courses the ridges of five mountains north of Harrisburg: Blue, Second, Sharp, Stony, and Peters mountains. You'll also be hiking on three of the major trails in eastern Pennsylvania—the Darlington, Horseshoe, and Appalachian trails. Even when elevation change is minimal the rocky ridges will slow your pace and hurt your feet.

As compensation, you'll have outstanding views of the Susquehanna and far-reaching mountains as far away as 25 miles, and a chance to explore land that remains much as it was when stagecoaches were common. You'll be miles away from civilization, forced to deal with the possibility of poisonous snakes and the scarcity of water. I carried two quarts of water on the hike: the best water sources are after the end of the second day, when you near the Appalachian Trail. If you have the right gear, a snowless winter would be ideal for this hike, when vistas expand through leafless trees. Fall is also excellent, if you are aware that you might run into hunters

as the trail passes through state game lands and state forest where hunting is allowed.

The trailhead is the Darlington Trail on the Susquehanna River about 2 miles north of Harrisburg just off US 22—US 322. Out of Harrisburg drive north on the River Road towards Fort Hunter. Turn right on PA 39, the Linglestown Road. Cross over the new US 322 and turn left on the first road that is not an entrance ramp to US 22—US 322. Bear left uphill almost immediately, following orange Darlington Trail blazes on telephone poles for 1 mile as you wind up Blue Mountain. The road turns right and ends .1 mile beyond, with pulloff space for one or two cars. The Darlington Trail leads off toward the very top of the mountain, on your left.

You should spot a second car at the end of the hike near Peters Mountain and the Clarks Ferry Bridge, about 8 miles north of PA 39 on US 22—US 322. Where US 22—US 322 turns left to cross the Susquehanna, continue straight ahead about 100 yards. The Appalachian Trail (AT) comes off Peters Mountain here to cross the river on the Clarks Ferry Bridge.

Parking is available anywhere on the right in a roomy pulloff.

If you are driving from the north, take US 11—US 15 south to the Clarks Ferry Bridge, where you cross the Susquehanna and spot your second car on the left before continuing south 8 miles to PA 39. From I-81 head south to exit 27, where you join PA 39 west 8 miles before turning right just before the US 22—US 322 entrance ramp. To spot the second car, join US 22—US 322 north 8 miles to the Clarks Ferry Bridge, then follow the rest of the driving instructions.

Day 1
Blue Mountain to
Horseshoe Trail
Total distance: 11.7 miles
Hiking time: 6½ hours
Vertical rise: 900 feet

Your first day is somewhat easier walking than the last two days of the trip. The early miles follow a woods road and other roads where you won't worry about rocks, and once you reach the crest of Blue Mountain, you follow it east almost all day, heading downhill only at Heckert and Manada gaps. Your route is the orange-blazed Darlington Trail, maintained by the Susquehanna Appalachian Trail Club. The entire trail is 25 miles long, beginning in Deans Gap (see Hike 26) at the junction of the Tuscarora and Appalachian trails. On the east side of the Susquehanna the trail follows Blue Mountain to the junction with the Horseshoe Trail, about 12 miles east.

Start walking left uphill where orange double blazes mark a turn. The trail climbs about 200 feet, indifferibly blazed until you reach the crest, but visibily worn as it switchbacks uphill. At .2 mile reach an overlook with excellent views of the Susquehanna, especially north to Fort Hunter just beyond the Rockville Bridge.

Although there is a small stone cairn here—a monument to Bishop Darlington, an early trail blazer—it has been vandalized.

At this point turn right to begin your trek along the crest on a pleasant, wide woods trail through pines and oaks. In early fall, squirrels and chipmunks continually scolded me as I walked past their dinner tables—flat rocks littered with half-eaten acorns in the middle of the trail. Notice also how steeply the narrow ridge falls away from you on either side. The mountains you'll traverse on this back-pack were all similarly formed by a folding action that heaved the land upward like a closed accordion.

At 1 mile cross a power-line cut with spectacular views south to Harrisburg and along the river to the right, with Second Mountain and its "antenna ranch" of local radio station towers on the left. Beyond, an extremely narrow paved road comes in from the left—used for access to a TV tower at 1.7 miles, not for regular traffic. Darlington Trail blazes are painted right on the road as it climbs uphill steadily.

At 1.7 miles take time to enjoy the spectacular view to the south, southwest, and southeast from the TV tower. Roundtop Ski Area, over 20 miles to the southeast, is in view, and you can see almost into Hershey, 25 miles away. The trail leaves the paved road and continues east along a wide cut .5 mile before entering dense oak woods again, where views are almost continuous after the leaves have fallen.

At 3 miles reach the mountain hollow Ungers Gap. Along this section, Delaware Indians and early eighteenth-century colonists had frequent, bloody dis-agreements that culminated in the French and Indian War in 1754. The contention here sprang from the Walking Purchase in 1737, a way of dividing territory that the Indians felt unfair. As a result a series of more than a dozen forts were built at 10- to 15-mile intervals from the Delaware River to the Susquehanna, many just south of the modern Appalachian Trail. The westernmost fort in this area was Fort Hunter, where a museum stands today. The lookout for Fort Hunter was up here on the ridge somewhere, possibly the site of the Darlington monument, although some local historians believe it was further east. Northing remains today of Fort Manada, near where you will camp tonight in Manada Gap.

Reach Pletz Pass at 4.7 miles, where an old woods road leads down to Linglestown on the right. From just beyond the pass to 7 miles into the hike, the path and mountain are peppered with Linglestown Rocks, a blocky outcropping along the mountain crest. Be especially watchful here for snakes—both poisonous and nonpoisonous. If you leave the trail to avoid rocks, be careful not to put your feet or hands on a ledge you can't see. A walking stick can be indispensable on this hike. It helps maintain your balance over small rocks that litter the path, and could help deflect a striking snake. I never backpack without my stick—a lightweight, old bamboo cross-country ski pole with leather hand loop and the bottom basket removed—which has served for everything from stream depth gauge to emergency tent pole.

At 8 miles begin a descent to Heckert Gap and Mount Laurel Church south of Piketown. At 9.1 miles you pass a few houses in the gap, cross a road, and immediately climb the ridge again, regaining 500 feet of altitude. At 11 miles begin a more severe descent to Manada Gap where you will camp for the night. There is no specific campsite in this area; before reaching the Horseshoe Trail at 11.7 miles, I set up my tent on a flat spot just off the trail, down from the windblown ridge.

Day 2
Horseshoe Trail
Total distance: 13 miles
Hiking time: 6 hours
Vertical rise: 1,500 feet

Although today's hike has more vertical rise than the other three days, I found it the easiest day of the trip. Most of the ups and downs are modest, on old woods roads and the Horseshoe Trail with footing easy enough for a horse and rider. Even a climb of 800 feet in 1.5 miles, to the western terminus of the Horseshoe Trail on the AT, seems easier on this wide, 120-mile trail that begins at Valley Forge.

The Darlington Trail ends at the Horseshoe Trail junction. To continue, turn left (north) on the Horseshoe Trail, and in .3 mile pass through the woods and fields of Manada Gap. From Manada Gap head back into mountains and forests, bypassing a series of faint woods roads and trails as you keep to the yellow-blazed Horseshoe Trail.

Your path crosses PA 443, then bears left along the edge of old fields at 1 mile. At 1.5 miles the trail bends left again, turning sharply right at 1.6 miles along the boundary of Fort Indiantown Gap Military Reservation. At 2.5 miles make a sharp right turn, following the boundary another 4.5 miles. Second Mountain looms above you on the left along the wooded, relatively flat trail.

At 7 miles the trail leaves the Indiantown Gap boundary and heads north again, up over the end of Second Mountain and across Stony Creek. At 7.8 miles reach the abandoned Schuylkill and Susquehanna railroad bed (see Hike 47), where you turn left onto the wide, gravel two-track. On the left is Stony Creek, a trout stream popular with fishermen. Along the edge hemlocks outnumber the oaks—and wood-sorrel, dog-toothed violets, and wild lily-of-the-valley hug the banks.

At 10.1 miles the trail leaves the easy

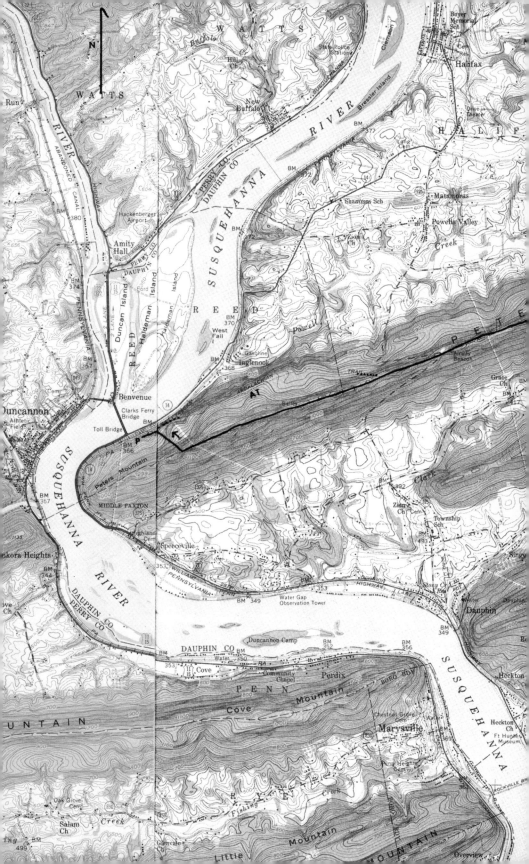

footing of the railroad bed to turn right, sharply uphill through Rattling Run Hollow. The Horseshoe Trail is wider, to accommodate the greater size of horses, and doesn't often climb at the severe angle of many hiking trails, but the ascent here is rocky and steep. At 10.3 miles an old woods road, now very faint, makes the nearly 800-foot elevation gain easier along this 1.5-mile section.

Climb up Sharp Mountain through a pretty hollow filled with hemlocks and large boulders. Where the Horseshoe Trail ends at the crest, turn left on the Appalachian Trail, then cross broad, flat Devils Race Course. On the other side at 11.5 miles, the AT climbs slightly, then descends. This side of the mountain is unexpectedly called Stony Mountain. For the hiker, there is almost no descent across the Devils Race Course—just a slight dip—but apparently that was enough for the mountains to receive different names.

After 1.5 miles on the AT, at 13 miles total, reach a spring (usually reliable) and a flat area where you can camp for the night. Tomorrow you'll finish the descent of Stony Mountain.

Day 3
Stony Mountain to Shaffer Shelter
Total distance: 8 miles
Hiking time: 5 hours
Vertical rise: 800 feet

This hiking day is short but tough—and includes a very difficult ascent over Peters Mountain. A hiker in excellent condition could probably finish the remaining 15.5 miles today, but the walk is more enjoyable if you add an extra day to your schedule. Since I hiked this section in late fall 1980, a forest fire swept across parts of Stony Mountain, destroying dozens of

acres. It is possible that the trail has been relocated around the fire damage.

Continue downhill on the AT with views north to DeHart Reservoir when the leaves are off the trees. At 1.7 miles turn to the right off the fire road at the bottom of the mountain and cross Clarks Creek. Just beyond, reach PA 325 and the game lands parking lot. Across PA 325 you start the steep climb up Peters Mountain. At 2.1 miles a blue-blazed side trail leads left a short distance to a good spring where you can refill your canteen. There is also water near the Shaffer Shelter tonight, so you might take only enough for today. (The spring is 400 yards down the side of the mountain from the shelter, however, so if you don't want to add that mileage to today's hike, you can fill up here and carry the extra weight.)

This climb is the most difficult of the hike, gaining 800 feet in 1 mile of narrow, steep, and rocky trail. Once at the top, you're hardly any better off—the trail continues west along the rocky ridge, rough going the entire way. Turn left when you crest Peters Mountain. At 3.8 miles on the left, the blue-blazed Shikellimy Trail heads back down the mountain to PA 325. Stay on the AT, reaching Shikellimy Rocks in .7 mile. Compensating for the rocky trail is a breathtaking view of the Susquehanna Valley and farmlands.

The rocks end in .3 mile, and at 7.8 miles the trail passes under a telephone cable where you again have good views north and south. Bear left on an abandoned road, which heads toward Powells Valley and Enterline to the right. Beyond a right bend is another blue-blazed side trail down to PA 325 —the Victoria Trail—so-called after an iron furnace functioning during the Revolutionary War.

At 8 miles reach the Earl Shaffer Shelter, named for the first person to hike the entire Appalachian Trail in a single season, the summer of 1948. Today, Shaffer is still an active member of the Susquehanna Appalachian Trail Club, based in Harrisburg. The blue-blazed trail to the spring heads off the north side of the mountain.

Day 4
Shaffer Shelter to Clarks Ferry Bridge
Total distance: 7.7 miles
Hiking time: 4 hours
Vertical rise: 300 feet

From the top of Peters Mountain—lined with monkey vines and mayapples among the rocks—it's a relatively easy walk back to your second car. There is no sustained climbing today, and the rocks beneath your feet will be your most persistent problem. Grouse and turkeys are likely sightings, but the few patches of green grass on the ridge do not look as if they've been grazed by deer.

At .9 mile on the right a blue-blazed trail leads down to Camp Hebron, a church camp. Table Rock is just beyond, about 20 feet off the trail on the left (good views), and Fumitory Rocks, another outcropping, is just past Table Rock. At 1.5 miles pass a shelter on the left. Cross PA 225 at 3.1 miles, then scramble up a steep bank—the only real climb of the day. Beyond is a jeep road along a pipeline clearing with good grassy footing.

In .3 mile turn right again, following a pipeline maintenance road to the ridge with good views ahead along the grassy two-track—a good place to spot grazing deer. At 4 miles turn left into the woods along the ridge top, on the same relocation of the AT as the Peters Mountain return (see Hike 24). (If you continue downhill instead, on the blue-blazed side trail—the old AT—the path to your car is easier. The old AT turns left on a woods road in 1 mile and rejoins the relocation near the Susquehanna Shelter.)

Continue along the AT on a narrow forest path across several pipelines and power cuts that afford increasingly better views as you near the mile-wide Susquehanna. At 6.9 miles turn right and descend sharply, reaching Susquehanna Shelter at 7 miles. Just beyond, cross the blue-blazed woods road (the old AT).

At 7.7 miles reach the bottom of Peters Mountain and your car on the right. This backpack is for experienced back-packers used to carrying thirty-five to forty pounds and coping with rocks, steep ascents, and occasional dry springs. Before hiking Five Mountains you must be in good condition. Several rugged day hikes like Peters Mountain, and a shorter but still challenging backpack like Caledonia to Pine Grove Furnace (see Hike 49), would be good warmups for this trip. If you regularly hike the trails in this book, you should be ready for the challenge of Five Mountains.

Guidebooks from Backcountry Publications

Written for people of all ages and experience, these highly popular and carefully prepared books feature detailed trail directions, notes on historical and natural points of interest, maps and photographs.

Fifty Hikes in Central Pennsylvania. By Tom Thwaites $6.95

Fifty Hikes in the Adirondacks. By Barbara McMartin $8.95

Fifty Hikes in New Hampshire's White Mountains. By Daniel Doan $7.95

Fifty More Hikes in New Hampshire. By Daniel Doan $6.95

Fifty Hikes in Vermont. By Ruth and Paul Sadlier $7.95

In the *Discover* **series—**

Discover the Adirondacks, 1: From Indian Lake to the Hudson River/A Four Season Guide to the Out-of-Doors. By Barbara McMartin $6.95

Discover the Adirondacks, 2: Walks, Waterways and Winter Treks in the Southern Adirondacks. By Barbara McMartin $7.95

In the *25 Walks* **series—**

25 Walks in the Finger Lakes Region (NY). By William P. Ehling $5.95

In the *Bike Tours* **series—**

20 Bicycle Tours in Vermont. By John Freidin $5.95

20 Bicycle Tours in New Hampshire. By Tom and Susan Heavey $5.95

In the *25 Ski Tours* **series—**

25 Ski Tours in Central New York. By William P. Ehling $5.95

25 Ski Tours in the Adirondacks. By Almy and Anne Coggeshall $5.95

25 Ski Tours in the Green Mountains (VT). By Sally and Daniel Ford $4.95

25 Ski Tours in the White Mountains (NH). By Sally and Daniel Ford. $4.95

In the *Canoeing* **series—**

Canoeing Central New York. By William P. Ehling $7.95

Canoeing Massachusetts, Rhode Island and Connecticut. By Ken Weber $6.95

Canoe Camping Vermont and New Hampshire Rivers. By Roioli Schweiker $4.95

Other outdoor recreation books—

Dan Doan's Fitness Program for Hikers and Cross-Country Skiers. By Daniel Doan $2.95

A Year with New England's Birds: A Guide to Twenty-Five Field Trips. By Sandy Mallett $2.95

Available from bookstores, sporting goods stores, or the publisher. For complete descriptions of these and all our recreational books, write to: Backcountry Publications, Inc., P.O. Box 175, Woodstock, Vermont 05091.